HUMAN MOTIVATION

Authors

Yoshio Kondo, *Professor Emeritus, Kyoto University*
Akikazu Kako, *Nippon Paint Co., Ltd.*
Junai Saito, *Sumitomo Heavy Industries, Ltd.*
Shozo Sakamoto, *Japan Inspection Co., Ltd.*
Shigeki Hayashi, *Sumitomo Heavy Industries, Ltd.*
Takeo Haruyama, *Sumitomo Jukikai Environment, Inc.*
Tai Michiura, *Amada Wasino Co., Ltd.*
Michiro Munechika, *Dai-ichi High Frequency Co., Ltd.*

HUMAN MOTIVATION

A Key Factor for Management

Edited by
Yoshio Kondo

3A Corporation
Tokyo, Japan

Originally published in Japan as *Ohanashi Mochibēshon* by Yoshio Kondo. ©Yoshio Kondo 1989, published by the Japanese Standards Association.

HUMAN MOTIVATION

©by 3A Corporation
Shoei Bldg., 6-3, Sarugaku-cho 2-chome, Chiyoda-ku, Tokyo 101, Japan

Translated by J.H. Loftus

First Printing 1991
Second Printing 1993

Printed in Japan

ISBN 4-906224-64-4

Foreword

L ast year, a friend of mine had the chance to visit and observe Company N, an American computer parts manufacturer. According to my friend, the president of this company was practicing management based on respect for humanity. All employees, including the president himself, were carrying out their jobs in close cooperation with each other. The company's productivity, therefore, was extraordinarily high, and it boasted excellent product quality. This was attested to by the fact that Apple Computers, which used the company's products, had praised them in the highest possible terms as the best available.

Company N's president claimed that his firm was exceptional in America, but it did not mean that they had adopted Japanese management practices. I think this shows that the type of management able to motivate employees transcends national boundaries and is the same the world over.

Written clearly and concisely, this book presents the results of many years of earnest discussion among the members of the Motivation Research Group led by Dr. Yoshio Kondo, Professor Emeritus, Kyoto University. It does not restrict itself to a narrow Japanese viewpoint but approaches the fundamentals of motivation through a searching examination of basic human nature.

I urge all business-people and managers to read this book.

March 1989   E. Eizaburo Nishibori

Editor's Preface

We are well aware that, in tackling a job, it is important to stimulate people's will to work, i.e., to motivate them. If a positive desire to do the work is lacking, people's valuable knowledge and intelligence will be wasted in thinking up excuses for not doing the task, and will be of no help in completing it.

How should we go about creating such a positive desire? Of course, patting people on the back and encouraging them is necessary, but motivation needs more than mere exhortation.

If asked whether there is an established, standardized methodology of motivation, like that which exists for statistical analysis, for example, we have to say that there is not. This is because the human beings whom we are trying to motivate are too diverse.

Nevertheless, we can discover many keys to motivation if we concentrate not on the differences in people's characters but on the common human traits that underlie these differences, i.e., human nature.

The Motivation Research Group, established at the Kansai Branch of the Japanese Standards Association on the recommendation of Dr. Eizaburo Nishibori and others, has been discussing these issues for many years. This book is a revised edition of a series of articles describing the results of these discussions published from January to December, 1988, in the magazine *Hyōjunka to Hinshitsu Kanri* (Standardization and Quality Control).

EDITOR'S PREFACE

The book consists of two main parts and an appendix.

Part 1, What Is Motivation?, contains twelve chapters on the basic, most important elements of motivation.

Part 2, Motivation in Industry, describes various case studies illustrating these elements. Since motivation can succeed only if all the basic, common, important elements are present, the case studies have been selected as comprehensive examples of the material presented in Part 1.

The appendix gives an outline of the motivation training course developed by the Motivation Research Group.

March 1989   Yoshio Kondo
                    Professor Emeritus, Kyoto University

Contents

Foreword   v

Editor's Preface   vii

Part 1 WHAT IS MOTIVATION?   1

1. Introduction   3
   Organizing Is Not Enough
   Motivation Theory as a Basis for Action
   Emphasize the Common Group
   The Social Problem of Motivation
   Superficial Measures Are Doomed to Fail
   Solutions Based on Root Causes
   What Is Work Apart From Money?

2. The Hierarchy of Human Needs   13
   Maslow's Hierarchy of Human Needs
   Herzberg's Motivation Theory
   Maslow and Herzberg Combined

3. What Is Work?   19
   A Critique of the Taylor System
   O'Toole's Definition of Work
   The Three Elements of Work

4. Work and Play   27
   Autonomy and Voluntariness

CONTENTS

The Unexpected
The Element of Tension
The Importance of Rhythm
Fair Comparisons
Immediate Results
Results Before Style
Effort and Skill
Achievement and Recognition
Results and Financial Rewards

5. Humanity   39
What Is Humanity?
Cerebral Physiology
The Three Elements of Work
Humanity and Human Nature

6. Ends and Means in Work   45
Work Attitudes and Responsibility
*Creativity—Mandatory Objectives, Optional
  Methods*
The Goal of Work—A Healthy Company

7. Creativity and Standardization   51
Creativity and Standardization
Work Standards
Must Means and Methods Be Obeyed?
Two Types of Work Standard

8. Breakthrough   59
*Production Cost and Defect Rate—Optimization or
  Breakthrough?*

CONTENTS

Preconditions for Breakthrough
Four Steps for Making Work More Creative

9. **Learning From Results**   **69**
Defects and Abnormalities
Praise and Blame
A Critique of Management by Objectives

10. **Teamwork**   **75**
Teamwork From the Outside
Reaching Out
Cooperation and Competition

11. **Leadership and Participation**   **83**
An Example
Leadership and Its Preconditions
Realizing Our Dreams
The Steps for Raising Ability
The Benefits of Participation
Real Participation

12. **Summary**   **91**
Human Motivation
Providing Satisfiers
The Three Elements of Work
Humanity and the Fun of Sports
A Sense of Responsibility
The Ends and Means of Work
Creativity
Teamwork, Leadership, and Participation
Conclusion

CONTENTS

Part 2   MOTIVATION IN INDUSTRY   101

Case Study 1

**Greater Motivation Through a Revitalized
Suggestion Scheme   103**

The History of Our Suggestion Scheme
Details of the Suggestion Scheme
Mechanisms for Invigorating Suggestion Schemes
Benefits and Costs
Future Topics

Case Study 2

Have People Sell a Dream   115

A Dream Takes Off—Encountering a Catalog
Making "Real Sake"
The Dream Is Achieved!

Case Study 3

**Engineer Motivation—An Enthusiastic
Development Team   121**

My View of Work as an Engineer
The Satisfaction of a Tough Fight
An Enthusiastic Development Team

Case Study 4

**A Production Section Manager's Battle
Notes   129**

Prolog
*No Company Goes Bust Because of Shirking
  Workers*
The Badger's Coming!
Wringing Out Grumbles

[xii]

CONTENTS

A Central Restroom and Tiled Bathroom
40% Investment Efficiency
QC Education for Foremen and Team Leaders
Epilog

Case Study 5
Drawing Out the Wisdom of the
Workplace   141
The Latent Power of the Workplace
Setting Up a Mechanism
Task Teams, QC Circles, and the Standing
  Organization
Complete Freedom in Methods
The Value of Interim Presentations
Creating a Partnership System for Cross-
  Cooperation

Case Study 6
Making Use of Teamwork   149
Introduction
Surface Defects on Steel Plate
Measures for Reducing Slab Defects
Establishing a Quality Control System
Summary

Case Study 7
Starting Up QC Circles   159
Introduction
Try It and See!
Trying Out My Ideas on QC

CONTENTS

*The Production Section Manager Is Suitably
  Impressed*
The Division Manager Fails to Understand
Reforming the Production Standards
Conclusion

Appendix
HUMAN MOTIVATION STUDY COURSE   **169**
Our Changing Times
Important Topics in Motivation
Response to Change
New Needs
Human Motivation Study Course
Motivation Systems
Motivation Methods
Carrying Out the Training

Bibliography   **185**

Part 1

WHAT IS MOTIVATION?

1. Introduction

Organizing Is Not Enough

Whatever type of work we are concerned with, motivating the people employed in it is one of the most vital of the many conditions and policies established to achieve our objectives—in fact, it is indispensable. We know that if the people involved in a task are sufficiently motivated, they can overcome all kinds of difficulties. The saying, "a company is its people" expresses this very well.

The more effort a company devotes to the development of new products and technology and to the associated quality assurance, the greater the scale of these activities becomes and the more areas they affect inside the company and the organizations it works with. When this happens, emphasis is placed on organizing and systematizing the work to avoid duplication of effort by different departments, to ensure that no necessary steps are omitted, and to strengthen interdivisional cooperative relations.

Will the task proceed smoothly as long as it is organized and systematized in this way? Not necessarily. In spite of an organization having been established, often the work does not seem to go well.

The danger arises that if work is highly organized in this way, people in the organization will become apathetic and lose their motivation. What we must do is clarify and put into practice the types of organization and operating methods that will preserve the positive attitude of those directly and indirectly employed in the task and stimulate their desire to work.

An ancient Japanese proverb reminds us that it is no good carving a Buddha but leaving out the spirit. However excellent an organization we create, it will be useless, or even counterproductive, if the people in it lack motivation.

Motivation Theory as a Basis for Action

So, what must we do in order to motivate our employees and stimulate their desire to work? Is such a thing in fact possible?

Some people claim it presumptuous to think that one human being can motivate another. While we must accept the existence of this contention, we are well aware that it does not alter the need for and importance of motivation. Those who make this kind of assertion prefer to use the word "encouragement" rather than "motivation."

We must also be careful how we use the word motivation, since it is sometimes used with pejorative connotations. Some people believe there are experts and techniques whose sole purpose is motivation and that these experts use their knowledge to make employees work harder without any benefit for the employees themselves. However, I do not believe that such motivation experts and techniques really exist; and if they do, I cannot believe that they would have any lasting effect.

Standardization is an effective means of disseminating various methods. The statistical methods used in quality control are one example of this; they enable calculations to be carried out according to a standardized procedure, e.g., for analysis of variance or regression analysis, and to be completed without error even when they are a little complicated. However, this kind of standardization is not equally effective in motivating people. We are all individuals with our own idiosyncrasies, and there are large variations in our characters and habits. A motivation procedure which suits one individual cannot always be expected to give the same results with another.

Some people claim that motivation is a matter of a person's frame of mind and that there is no logic behind it. They say that, like putting the spirit into the Buddha, it is enough just to deal with people sincerely and openly, and they therefore restrict themselves to exhortation alone. While it is certainly true that motivation means moving people's hearts and minds, and that this is impossible if we do not deal with them fairly, this is a different question from that of whether or not a logical theory of motivation exists. Such a theory definitely does exist, and it is vital to base our actions on it firmly.

Emphasize the Common Ground

When discussing motivation, some people emphasize differences, such as those between the developing and the developed nations, between Japan, America, and Europe, etc. However, we do not take that standpoint here.

If we concentrate exclusively on differences, we may have to concern ourselves not only with, for example, the different management styles in Japan and America, but also with differences between companies in the same country and even with differences between workplaces in the same company and individuals in the same workplace. Discussion that emphasizes such differences often winds up in a blind alley in which "cultural disparities" or "personality clashes" are cited, which is of no help at all in solving practical problems.

We in the Motivation Research Group actively search out points in common rather than look for differences as described above. In other words, we search out the common important elements relating to motivation, and this is the aim of the present book.

It is as if we are about to analyze a given set of figures into their prime numbers, not with the aim of emphasizing their differences, but to find their greatest common divisor. As this book will show, this greatest common divisor (i.e., the common important elements) is surprisingly large.

The Social Problem of Motivation

As I have mentioned, motivation is a vital, indispensable condition for achieving work objectives, and people have stressed the importance of this awareness for years.

However, motivating company employees only began to become a serious problem in the advanced Western nations from about the beginning of the 1970s, and it is therefore not such an old problem after all.

In retrospect, we can see a sudden change as we left the prosperous 1960s and entered the 1970s. A number of social problems had already begun to surface at the start of the decade; the following three are often quoted as typical examples:

(1) Student unrest
(2) Product liability
(3) Motivation

At first glance, it is easy to consider these problems completely different phenomena. However, they all have the same roots and a high degree of commonality. All are closely related to the rise in our living standards and educational levels. It goes without saying that improvements in living standards and education are a desirable social trend, but we

Introduction

should also be aware that they are accompanied by a greater possibility of the occurrence of the social problems mentioned above.

Let us consider problems (2) and (3), the two most directly related to quality control.

The question of product liability, which is having such profound effects on American society, is considered to have arisen through a combination of the increase in the variety of products used in domestic households resulting from increasingly affluent lifestyles, a change in the social climate as the emphasis switched from establishing an industrial state to protecting consumers, the huge numbers of lawyers in America, and the system of trial by jury. This type of problem is now becoming even more severe, not only in manufacturing but also in service industries and the medical field.

Concerning the problem of motivation, many employees of companies in the advanced Western nations have become

[7]

disenchanted, as their lives have become more affluent, with the monotonous work that subdivision of labor has given them. As pay levels have risen, they have opted for more time off to enjoy their lives rather than higher incomes.

As a result, the absentee rate in companies has risen dramatically and has even reached as high as 10% to 20%, depending on the country, the company, and changes in the business climate. This rise in absenteeism is not merely decreasing production volumes, but is also seriously affecting product quality.

When the absentee rate goes up, it becomes particularly high on Fridays and Mondays, on either side of the weekend. In America, cars which are particularly fault-ridden are jokingly called "FM cars" (cars made on a Friday or Monday) or "night-shift cars."

Superficial Measures Are Doomed to Fail

As part of its employee motivation policy, Sweden's automobile manufacturer Volvo has built a completely new kind of assembly plant at the old port town of Kalmar, facing the Baltic Sea. The external appearance of the hexagonal factory building is sufficiently surprising to visitors, but entering the extremely quiet interior with its total absence of conveyor belts is just like stepping straight into the 21st century. Instead of conveyors, this factory uses large numbers of battery-powered, radio-controlled carts on which the cars are assembled. The idea is to give employees a wider range of jobs and much more freedom of action, thereby raising their interest and stimulating their desire to work. Volvo has shown commendable zeal and ability in planning and constructing such a factory, but there are various problems. The hoped-

Down with Inhuman
Productivity Rises!

for results are not being obtained, and those responsible say
they are having a hard time.

Some companies have proposed changing the present
40-hour, 5-day work week to a 40-hour, 4-day week. While
it is generally a desirable thing to increase the number of
days off in a week, this proposal is actually said to be a meas-
ure for dealing with the rapidly-increasing absentee rate on
Fridays. I believe that simply reducing the 5-day work week
to four days without tackling the source of the problem is
no more than inviting an increase in the absentee rate on
Thursdays.

Full-scale production of compact cars started in America around 1970. The aim was to stave off the avalanche of
imported compact cars from Japan and Europe coming on
to the American domestic market, which was very promis-
ing at that time, and to maintain and expand market share.
General Motors, America's biggest car manufacturer,

planned and designed a compact car called the Vega, with higher performance than the equivalent imported models, and started production at a new plant in Lordstown, Ohio. To cut costs through better productivity, a policy of automating production by shortening the manufacturing process and introducing industrial robots was adopted. At the same time, the company employed large numbers of young workers and paid them a high daily wage. Using such measures, it was able to start production at the astonishingly high rate of 120 units per hour.

Unfortunately, these labor policies aimed at achieving high productivity did not succeed. Soon after the plant began operating, the employees started a long-drawn-out strike under the slogan, "Down With Inhuman Productivity Rises." The quality of the Vega cars the factory produced was also worse than expected, and many had to be recalled, mainly because of the employees' lack of skill and motivation.

Also, it was reported that although this factory worked a 5-day week, a young worker ended up saying that he would come to work just four days a week, but only because he could not afford to eat if he came less often.

Solutions Based on Root Causes

Although the sorts of problems described above, now surfacing in America and Europe, are not so serious in Japan, Japan is not totally insulated from them.

I do not think such problems can be solved by superficial measures such as replacing the production-line system with some other system or giving employees longer weekends. Only solutions based on searching out and clarifying the true causes of these phenomena will be real and lasting.

We are very fortunate in Japan in having a uniform society consisting of people of the same race speaking the same language. The lack of serious motivation problems in Japan is probably due partly to the social environment. However, I believe we should not simply sit back and enjoy the benefits of our society; as well as identifying and utilizing the common important elements of motivation which have been nurtured here, we have a responsibility to communicate them to the rest of the world.

What Is Work Apart From Money?

Let us think about the relationship between our work and money. When we are poor, the relation between work and money is extremely close because human beings usually need money for food and clothes in order to live. However, as our lifestyles become more affluent and society matures, the value of money in relation to work decreases rapidly. If, in spite of this, we persist in the belief that work consists of nothing more than earning money, it will lead to an increase in the absentee rate.

We need money in order to live. But is our work really nothing more than a way of making money? Clearly, the answer is no. What is it apart from money which spurs us on to do good, worthwhile work? The answer to this question is the key to understanding motivation.

The problem of motivation becomes more and more difficult as our living standards and educational levels rise. In ten years, we will enter the 21st century, and our society will have developed even beyond the point where it is today. When this happens, there is no doubt that there will be an increasing emphasis on the same problem, albeit in different guise.

2. The Hierarchy of Human Needs

Motivation theories take human desire as their subject of study. Among the best-known and most typical examples of these are Maslow's hierarchy of human needs and Herzberg's motivation theory, together with McGregor's Theory Y.

Maslow's Hierarchy of Human Needs

The hierarchy of human needs proposed by A.H. Maslow in 1943 when he was a Professor of Psychology at Massachusetts Institute of Technology is well known. It is cited in many books and is usually described as shown in Fig. 1.1(a). Human needs are explained as being divided into the following:

(1) Physiological needs
(2) Safety needs
(3) Social needs
(4) Ego or esteem needs
(5) Self-fulfillment needs

These needs form a hierarchy ranging from physiological needs at the bottom to self-fulfillment needs at the top. Starting with physiological needs, when one need is satisfied, the need at the next higher level arises to replace it. Following this hierarchy, human needs are shown to manifest themselves in step-wise fashion.

For example, a typical physiological need is our appetite

[13]

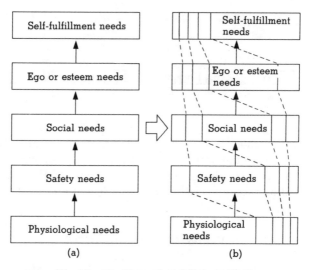

Fig. 1.1   The Hierarchy of Human Needs

for food, which prevents us from starving. We must obtain food in order to live, and this is why we work and earn money. In other words, when we are poor, we work in order to satisfy our appetite for food; but when we have satisfied our appetite in this way, we turn to the need at the next higher level, the need for safety.

At first glance, this explanation seems plausible, but we are left wondering whether poor people work only to satisfy their physiological needs. Those of us in the older generation in Japan experienced the years of terrible poverty immediately after the Second World War, when we had to work hard simply to fill our bellies. However, it would be untrue to say that we did not search for ways to satisfy our higher-level needs; we did our best even on empty stomachs.

When we take this into account, it is clear that the previous interpretation of Maslow's hierarchy of human needs is wrong. In fact, what Maslow stressed in his original paper was that human needs do not ascend the hierarchy in orderly succession; all five needs are always present, but their relative importance gradually shifts from lower to higher levels as our living standard rises, as shown in Fig. 1.1(b). In thinking about motivation, it is important to remember that human beings always have a variety of needs.

Herzberg's Motivation Theory

According to the motivation theory proposed by Professor Frederick Herzberg of the University of Chicago in 1969, motivation is governed by two different types of factor, which he named satisfiers and dissatisfiers.

For example, we feel dissatisfaction with things such as low pay or an overheated or noisy working environment, and

it is important and effective to eliminate such dissatisfiers by measures such as raising pay, installing air conditioners, or improving working conditions and employee facilities. However, simply removing sources of dissatisfaction will not necessarily motivate us and stimulate our desire to work.

To motivate us, it is essential to provide our daily work with another type of factor: satisfiers. Satisfiers extremely effective in motivating people include involving employees in preparing work standards and setting work goals, accurately appraising their results, and rewarding them appropriately.

Satisfying the relatively low-level needs in Maslow's human needs hierarchy shown in Fig. 1.1, such as physiological and safety needs, can be thought of as equivalent to removing dissatisfiers such as hunger or cold, whereas meeting the higher-level needs requires the provision of satisfiers.

Maslow and Herzberg Combined

When we look at things in this way, it is obvious that we cannot be motivated merely by satisfying our physiological and safety needs, for example. It is also clearly wrong to regard human needs as arising in orderly succession as each lower-level need is satisfied, as indicated by Fig. 1.1(a). The five types of need are always present; and, although it is also important to satisfy lower-level needs (i.e., to remove dissatisfiers), meeting higher-level needs by providing suitable satisfiers is crucial to motivation.

We are normally quick to identify dissatisfiers when we come across them, but we usually have only a hazy idea of the reasons for our dissatisfaction when satisfiers are absent. This is probably because dissatisfiers are more closely related to our basic survival instincts.

[16]

The Hierarchy of Human Needs

Although both dissatisfiers and satisfiers are important for motivation, providing suitable satisfiers is probably a more vital question because of the greater difficulty of recognizing them.

3. What Is Work?

A Critique of the Taylor System

At the beginning of the 1970s, when absentee rates began to rise and motivation started to become a problem, Dr. Juran published a series of articles in the American journal *Quality Progress* entitled "The Taylor System and Quality Control." In the first article, published in May 1973, Juran stated the following:

"Early in the 20th century, an American engineer, Frederick W. Taylor, proposed a revolutionary approach to management, based on his experience as a manager and as a consultant. Taylor's proposals may be summarized as follows:

- the methods for doing work should be based on scientific study, not on the empirical judgment of foremen or workmen
- the standards of what constitutes a day's work should likewise be based on scientific study
- selection and training of workmen should also be based on scientific study
- piece work payment should be employed to motivate selected and trained workmen to use the engineered methods and to meet the standards of a day's work.

"To make these proposals effective, Taylor separated work planning from its execution. Next, he created industrial engineers and other specialists to prepare work methods and

Part 1: WHAT IS MOTIVATION?

standards of a day's work. He then limited the foremen and workmen to 'control,' i.e., to execute the plans and meet the standards. The system 'worked'—it achieved spectacular improvements in productivity. Under Taylor's competent advocacy, the system was widely adopted by American industry, took firm root, and remains as the principal base on which our managerial structures have been erected.

"Now, more than half a century later, we are able to identify with clarity the then-existing premises behind the Taylor system:

- the foremen and workmen of that day lacked the technological literacy needed to plan work methods, to establish standards of a day's work, etc.
- the standard of living was so low that piece work incentives could provide a powerful stimulus to employees to meet standards

• the economic power of the employers was sufficient to prevail over employee resistance to such a system of management.

These premises were quite valid in Taylor's day, but they have since become increasingly obsolete. Today's foremen and workmen are well educated, including education in technology. Rising standards of living have sharply diminished the influence of piece work as an incentive to productivity. The rise of labor unions has required that many decisions affecting productivity be based on collective bargaining rather than on unilateral planning.

"Despite this obsolescence of Taylor's premises, we retain the Taylor system, with all the detriments inherent in the use of a system which is based on obsolete premises. The most obvious and serious of these detriments is the underemployment of the intelligence and creative capacity of millions of human beings."

As mentioned in Chapter 1, the idea that work is nothing more than a means of earning money is widespread in advanced Western nations. Let us consider the work of a housewife from this standpoint.

A housewife is responsible for a great variety of jobs around the home, including cleaning and tidying, training and educating her children, preparing meals and clearing up afterward, and washing and ironing. She works from dawn to dusk on behalf of her family. But housewives do not get paid for their work. If we define work as being merely something one does for money, we reach the startling conclusion that housewives do not work. In fact, there is an increasing tendency in the Western advanced nations for married women to employ someone else to do their housework while they themselves take outside jobs in order to earn money.

O'Toole's Definition of Work

In America in the 1970s, as the social climate began to change and people started to make points like the above, greater attention was paid to how people worked. The federal government formed a task force chaired by J. O'Toole and entrusted it with investigating the problem. After two years, in 1973, the task force published its findings under the title "Work in America."

In this well-known report, O'Toole criticized the American custom of emphasizing the relationship between work and financial compensation. He proposed that work be defined as "An activity that produces something of value for other people."

Although this definition was not universally accepted in America, it describes the job of a housewife perfectly.

The Three Elements of Work

Meanwhile, Dr. Nishibori, as discussed in more detail in Chapter 5, stresses that human work should always include the following three elements:

(1) Creativity (the joy of thinking)
(2) Physical activity (the joy of physical work)
(3) Sociality (the joy of sharing pleasure and pain with colleagues)

Positive feedback of these three elements is shown by the arrows in Fig. 1.2.

Although O'Toole's and Nishibori's proposals were made

[22]

What Is Work?

Fig. 1.2 The Three Elements of Work

independently, they match each other perfectly if we interpret O'Toole's definition in the following way:

An activity   *(physical activity)*
that produces something of value   *(creativity)*
for other people   *(sociality)*

Together, these proposals exemplify the true nature of human work.

Let us consider the Taylor method of working mentioned earlier. Taylor separated work into planning and execution and entrusted the former to specialists, on the premise that in those days workers at the foreman or operator level were of low ability and did not have the necessary skills to plan their work and establish standards. This meant that much of the creativity of foremen and operators was ignored.

Work was certainly a physical activity, but its social aspect was also ignored, since it was based on the piecework system and was therefore evaluated in monetary terms.

Working under conditions in which the creative and social aspects of their work were ignored, many employees, as their living standards improved, became disenchanted with their standardized, subdivided, monotonous tasks. And, as their wages rose, they began to want more time off to enjoy their lives in preference to higher wages. The resulting increase in absenteeism was the natural outcome.

Some people take the view that work is hard and it should therefore be rewarded by an amount of money appropriate to the pain involved. While we certainly need money in order to live, the question is whether people will be strongly motivated to work if their efforts are rewarded only with money.

Let us recall the human satisfiers and dissatisfiers mentioned in Chapter 2. Although money accepted as remuneration for work may alleviate or eliminate some of our dissatisfiers, it obviously cannot supply us with all the satisfiers we require.

The intangible rewards provided by work, such as creating something, however humble, experiencing the pleasure of sharing with colleagues, and taking pride in one's work, are extremely valuable.

4. Work and Play

Although earning money is not our only reason for working, in hard times when our living standards are low, work and money are very closely linked. Work is then regarded simply as a way of making money, while leisure is something which uses it up. We work because otherwise we would starve.

However, as educational levels rise and living standards improve, the value of the money we receive for our work diminishes rapidly; a person whose wages are doubled does not need to eat enough for two or wear two suits of clothes. The rise in absenteeism in advanced Western nations described in Chapter 1 is a manifestation of this.

As work and money become more and more separate, the distinction between work and leisure blurs and the two begin to overlap. The recent boom in the leisure and fashion industries is an example of this, and it has become difficult to distinguish clearly between work and leisure in these areas. This kind of change can be regarded as a phenomenon typifying the maturation of a society.

One typical leisure activity is sports. It is a commonly accepted idea that, while work may sometimes be unpleasant, sports are such fun that they can almost make one forget about eating and sleeping. Today, as the line between work and play becomes harder to define, it is important for us to find out why this should be so.

If we could identify the elements that make sports enjoyable and take positive steps to incorporate them into our work, work would become more pleasurable. What exactly are the pleasures of sports? I think some of them are as described below.

Autonomy and Voluntariness

Professional sports may seem very glamorous to the outsider, but I doubt whether they are as enjoyable to those actually engaged in them. The reason we amateurs feel that sports are fun is that we indulge in them voluntarily and on our own terms.

As paid employees, we perform work which has been allocated to us. How can we convince ourselves that we are doing this work not under compulsion from our superiors or from those around us but of our own free will? Some people find that they can actually stop themselves from feeling seasick by imagining that it is not the ship which is rocking them, but they who are rocking the ship.

In QC circle activities, autonomy and voluntariness are given top priority. The mistaken idea that, because QC circles are voluntary, managers should adopt a laissez-faire attitude toward them has now vanished. The desire of QC circles to leave no stone unturned in investigating a topic which they themselves have selected stems from their voluntary nature. It is also widely recognized as being extremely valuable.

The Unexpected

In sports, things do not always turn out as expected, and this is what makes them fun. There would be nothing more boring than a sport which was either completely predictable or completely unpredictable.

A copper refinery on the shore of the Seto Inland Sea in Japan installed the latest type of flash smelter and adopted a high level of computer control. As the compositions of the matte and slag discharged from the furnace were important characteristic values for controlling the process, samples were taken at regular intervals and were analyzed by female employees (technical-college graduates) in the refinery's laboratory using X-ray fluorescence analysis equipment. Since this equipment was extremely expensive, only designated female workers were allowed to handle it.

The female employees could not work on the night shift, and samples taken during the night were not analyzed until the following morning. However, it was inconvenient for the smelter operators to have to wait for the results, so it was decided to allow the night-shift operators to use the equipment and analyze the samples themselves. This bold decision triggered a boost in workplace morale.

The smelter operators were allowed to adjust the operating conditions within certain limits, and they were extremely happy to be able to analyze the matte and slag compositions themselves and find out immediately whether the conditions they had set were right. They were delighted if the results matched their predictions and very keen to know why if they did not.

The result was that the operators became eager to study the process more deeply and understand it for themselves. The refinery management encouraged them by arranging seminars and study groups. The upshot was that operator morale increased by leaps and bounds.

It is vital to find out how we can stimulate our thirst for knowledge and desire for improvement in this way.

The Element of Tension

Sports are fun because they occasionally create tension. Predictability would eliminate the element of tension in a sport, and make it extremely dull. On the other hand, we would find a sport unbearable if it kept us in a constant state of tension from start to finish.

So, what is the best way of incorporating a certain amount of tension into our work from time to time? There are various methods we can try.

The Importance of Rhythm

Every sport has its own particular rhythm, and so does work. The actions of the barber snipping the air briskly with his scissors when cutting a customer's hair or the ticket inspector clicking his ticket punch rapidly in the intervals between clipping tickets can be thought of as ways of keeping a steady rhythm.

When the rate of production of a manufacturing process is increased, it is natural to fear an increase in the number of nonconforming products because of the increased speed of the line. But we would be wrong to assume that the number of nonconforming products will decrease when the rate of production is reduced and the line is slowed down; in fact, the number of nonconforming products often increases. This can be explained as the result of a disturbance in the rhythm of the work.

It is therefore important to maintain a steady rhythm of work. However, various external factors often tend to upset the rhythm even when workers are eager to do their best; for example, raw materials or parts may fail to arrive when needed or may include large numbers of nonconforming items, or machines may repeatedly malfunction because of inadequate preventive maintenance. We should also be aware that factors disturbing the rhythm of work may be introduced by managers or staff as well as by the workers themselves.

Fair Comparisons

In both individual and team sports, the results are soon made known to the players and provide a fair basis of comparison. This is one of the pleasurable elements of sports and has helped give rise to the notion of fair play.

In a word, the fun of sports lies in the fact that we take part in them voluntarily, that the results give a fair comparison of our ability, and that we cannot be sure whether we will win or lose.

Some sports, such as golf, have a handicapping system which allows beginners to play experienced players with an equal chance of winning. Such devices are used because the fairness of comparison is important, although there will always be somebody who will claim that the handicapping was unfair. People naturally tend to look for an excuse when they lose. So, can we not make fair comparisons without the use of handicaps? In many cases we can, by using the orthogonal principle, one of the most important principles in the design of experiments.

Fairness is important in sports and work because it stimulates our competitive spirit. Whether we are aware of it or not, this competitive spirit is very strong in human beings and must be handled carefully.

Part 1: WHAT IS MOTIVATION?

Some people believe that comparing results only invites discontent and can lead to the situation getting out of hand. However, this is often because they have confused the comparison of results with the subsequent evaluation of performance. When the result of a match is known, the loser acknowledges defeat and vows to win the next time. However, the loser is bound to become aggrieved if, like kicking someone who is down, we then proceed to criticize the person for losing.

Long-term evaluations must be carried out with strict impartiality, but the short-term, day-to-day evaluations we are talking about here should, I believe, lean more toward the elements of humor and encouragement.

Immediate Results

In many sports, the result is known right away. In tenpin bowling, for example, the bowlers know how many pins they

have knocked down as soon as they have bowled. Imagine what a boring game it would be if they had to wait two or three days or even until the end of the month to discover their scores. Finding out the results without delay is one of the things that makes sports interesting.

What about work? It is true to say that the results of workers' efforts are rarely immediately apparent and they often have to wait two or three days at best, or sometimes even longer, to check the outcome. As our discussion of sports shows, this tends to rob our work of interest.

We ourselves should promptly check the quality of the products we have made. Or, as soon as the quality of a product from a previous process becomes apparent in a subsequent process, we should let the person who made the product know. This is one of the secrets of making work interesting.

One method of notifying people of the results of their work is, as in the use of "defect bulletins," to inform them only of their slip-ups. But this type of feedback would be like saying to sports players, "We'll let you know if you've lost, but not if you've won. If you don't hear anything, you can assume that you've won." Surely we should do the opposite, and tell the winner that he has won. We should inform our operators right away, with much fanfare, if they have produced a perfect batch of products.

Results Before Style

In most sports, apart from those such as gymnastics, we are concerned solely with winning or losing, and it does not matter whether a person looks good or not, provided he or she obeys the rules of the game.

The important thing in manufacturing is to make defect-

free products, and there is no point in following the operating standards if doing so results in nothing but defectives.
I am not saying that we do not need standards or that we do
not have to obey them, but that it is the standards themselves
which are the problem.

Work standards consist of the following three parts:

(1) Objectives
(2) Constraints
(3) Standard motions

These are discussed in more detail in Chapter 7, but we
can note here that "objectives" must be achieved by whoever
is doing the work, and everyone must obey "constraints." The
problem lies in the third part, "standard motions." Unlike
constraints, these are not something which everyone must
obey without fail. Since they are standards for action, there
can be any number of "applied actions" which make use of
them.

As the saying "many men, many minds" suggests, we are
all individuals and all have our own particular foibles and
idiosyncrasies. Trying to force everyone to follow the same
standards will have the opposite of the intended effect,
upsetting the rhythm of work and leading to more defects
and lower efficiency. Just try making a left-hander follow a
standard written for right-handers!

Instead, either on our own or working with others, we
should utilize these standard motions to create the applied
actions which best suit each individual.

To use the analogy of sports once more: when learning
a sport, we have to start by mastering the basic movements,
but we must use this as a foundation on which to improve
our performance through daily sweat and toil.

Effort and Skill

In sports, our score depends on our own effort and skill. This is why we get angry with ourselves when we do badly and why we strive to do better. Also, as mentioned before, we soon find out when our efforts are rewarded.

Exactly the same thing applies to work. So, how can we go about building into the workplace a mechanism which will allow each individual's skill and effort to be reflected in the results of his or her work and ensure that everyone experiences this together with their colleagues? One thing is clear: it is extremely difficult to do so in a Taylor-style workplace like that depicted in Charlie Chaplin's movie *Modern Times*.

Creativity is important in any workplace, but we must make sure that there is a proper outlet for it. In sports, for example, it is exciting to try and win by seeing how well you can fool the umpire and bend the rules. However, this type of creativity is clearly out of order. The only permissible kind of creativity in sports is the kind exercised within the rules in the spirit of fair play. In work, the constraints mentioned previously correspond to the rules in sports.

Achievement and Recognition

When we achieve a good score in a sport, we brag about it to our friends. Even if we keep quiet about it, our friends will probably accept the results without quibbling and congratulate us on them. This makes us very happy. Conversely, we feel very ashamed if our friends jeer at us for losing.

Comparisons in sports are always impartial, and, as discussed below, the results in amateur sports are not directly linked with money. This is why amateur sports promote the spirit of fair play and true camaraderie among players.

While it is not pleasant to be bawled out by our boss for making a mistake at work, it is even worse to be cold-shouldered by our colleagues. This means that work is not just something we do for money but rather it is based on the strong desire to be useful to and please our peers.

Results and Financial Rewards

In amateur sports, the results are not directly money-related, and this is another important element in making sports fun. It also has a strong bearing on the system of rewards in a company. Although in Japanese companies, employees or groups of employees are often rewarded with gifts of money, this is not a very good way of praising them.

It is more important to devise effective ways of rewarding people which do not involve money.

One company has adopted the following method of rewarding its employees. To begin with, company regulations make it the duty of the president to attend company QC circle conferences and of the operations division managers to attend divisional conferences. As the date of a conference approaches, the QC promotion office prepares a Polaroid camera, photograph albums, and a felt-tipped pen, but not just for presentation as prizes.

Once the conference has started, each presentation is photographed, and the photograph is mounted at the top of the first page of an album. The president then uses the pen to write a short note of thanks under the photograph and awards the album to the circle at the end of the presentation.

This method of commendation is a reward system which cannot be bought with money. However, its effectiveness is rather short-lived and it cannot be used forever. Much effort must be made to devise new methods of showing appreciation to employees. Often, just a word from a thoughtful manager who values his subordinates can be a tremendous encouragement.

5. Humanity

As discussed in the previous chapter, work is sometimes not very enjoyable, but sports are usually tremendous fun. The various pleasures that sports afford can be summed up by saying that sports are enjoyable because they always contain the element of humanity, while work is sometimes unenjoyable because it has become dehumanized to a certain extent.

Much emphasis is placed on respect for humanity these days, and the word "humanity" crops up frequently in our daily conversation. However, there is little discussion of what humanity actually is, and I think that our understanding of it is still inadequate.

The study of the essence of humanity is an important pursuit in philosophy and psychology, but many academics concentrate on the metaphysical approach, and elucidating the nature of humanity is considered to be extremely difficult. People are often said to be irrational creatures.

Nevertheless, humanity is closely related to the nature of work and motivation, and I will therefore be so bold as to consider it from two or three different aspects.

What Is Humanity?

According to the Concise Oxford Dictionary, humanity means "being human" or "human attributes." However, there is no explanation of what human attributes are or what it means to be human. At any rate, we soon realize the limitations of dictionaries in helping us to understand what humanity is.

The explanations given in dictionaries can be interpreted in various ways, but I think we can use them to define humanity as those unique qualities which characterize humans and set them apart from other animals.

To begin with, any explication of motivation or humanity must be an explication of the workings of the human heart and mind. These in turn depend on the workings of our brain and not on those of our physical heart, which is no more than a pump for circulating the blood.

Cerebral Physiology

Cerebral physiology is a field of study that attempts to elucidate the workings of the brain. Investigations include comparing the structure of the human brain with the brains of other animals, and observing the functional impact caused by changes in specific parts of the brain. This approach is thus more amenable to scientific proof than the metaphysical approach of philosophers and psychologists, and is easier for us to understand.

In his book *Ningen de Aru Koto* ("Being Human"), the cerebral physiologist Professor T. Tokizane cites the twenty-six items listed in Table 1.1 as the features which characterize human beings. Higher-order animals closely related to human beings, such as chimpanzees, gorillas, and Japanese monkeys, are known to possess most of these features, and they are therefore not exclusive to humans. We would be overrating humans if we thought so. Although the features

Humanity

Table 1.1 Being Human

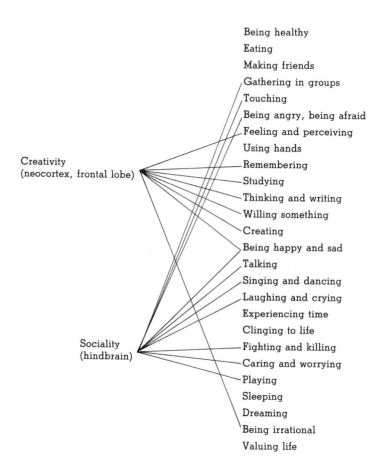

Being healthy
Eating
Making friends
Gathering in groups
Touching
Being angry, being afraid
Feeling and perceiving
Using hands
Creativity (neocortex, frontal lobe)
Remembering
Studying
Thinking and writing
Willing something
Creating
Being happy and sad
Talking
Singing and dancing
Laughing and crying
Experiencing time
Clinging to life
Sociality (hindbrain)
Fighting and killing
Caring and worrying
Playing
Sleeping
Dreaming
Being irrational
Valuing life

are seen in animals other than humans, we are justified in saying that humans possess them to a far greater degree.

[41]

Part 1: WHAT IS MOTIVATION?

Most of the features listed in Table 1.1 can be broadly classified into three types: those concerned with creativity (mainly connected with that part of the brain including the frontal lobe known as the cerebrum); those concerned with sociality (mainly connected with the part of the brain called the hindbrain); and the rest. In other words, the main elements which constitute humanity are as follows:

1) Creativity
2) Sociality
3) Others

The Three Elements of Work

As discussed in Chapter 3, Nishibori's and O'Toole's proposals show that our work must always incorporate the following three elements:

1) Creativity
2) Activity
3) Sociality

Since work naturally involves activity, we can summarize the above discussion by saying that fully exercising our humanity in our work is essential for motivation.

If this is true, the key to motivating people lies in incorporating and making use of the elements of humanity, i.e., creativity, sociality, and the rest, in our daily work. The following chapters concentrate particularly on how to build the element of creativity into work.

Humanity and Human Nature

One further point should be made. According to Tokizane, the structure of the human brain is exactly the same in all human beings and is completely unrelated to race, skin color, sex, or other differences. In addition, the humanity we have been discussing, which originates in the structure and function of the human brain, has evolved together with the development of humankind over an extremely long period, since man first appeared on the surface of the earth over a million years ago. This means that, even if superficial social customs change, the current of humanity which runs beneath these changes will not alter markedly in a short period of time.

Through exercising their natural gift of humanity to the full, our ancestors did what other animals were unable to do: they created civilization on the earth. I believe it is vital, in whatever age we find ourselves, to make full use of our humanity, and not just the acquisition of money, as the driving force behind our work.

6. Ends and Means in Work

The most important thing when we are working, whether we are doing a job ourselves or getting colleagues or subordinates to do it, is to achieve the true aims of the work. One of the preconditions for succeeding in this is that everyone involved should have had these true aims clearly explained to them and that they all understand and accept the importance of achieving them.

Work Attitudes and Responsibility

Generally speaking, everyone has a different approach to getting other people to do work. Two typical approaches are

1) Employing people in place of machines
2) Employing people to use machines

The first of these approaches is centered around machines, while the second is people-centered.

The standpoint of the first approach is that, unlike machines, people easily become bored with their work and are liable to become dissatisfied; it would therefore be better to automate the work. This would be difficult in many cases because of a lack of technical capabilities or finances, and there is no choice but to use human labor.

In the planning phase of a job, the real aims of the work are clarified and instructions are given as to the means and methods to be used for achieving the aims. However, adopting the first of the above standpoints makes it unnecessary to inform people of the true aims of the work. When people are being used as a substitute for machines, a detailed explanation of the means and methods to be used is far more important than a description of the objectives to be attained; in fact, it is indispensable.

Suppose that workers have only been informed of the means and methods of doing the job, and that all the products they make turn out to be nonconforming. The managers who gave the instructions will almost certainly rush to the workplace and blame the workers, claiming that they are responsible for producing the nonconforming items. When scolded like this, the workers can quite reasonably reply that they carried out the work faithfully according to the instructions they had been given and that, if nonconformance resulted, it was because the instructions were incorrect and it was not their fault. In fact, this is a common occurrence.

A strong sense of responsibility toward work cannot be created by treating people as a substitute for machines and telling them only how to do the work but not its purpose.

The second standpoint is that, however mechanized and automated a process has become, it is ultimately human beings who use the machines to get the job done. The work revolves around people. If we adopt this standpoint, the training and education of those people assumes importance; but, over and above this, it is also easy to see that it is essential to state clearly the true aims of the work, so that the people responsible for performing it can think how best to achieve them.

We tend to think that we have taken the best course of action if we clearly inform people of the true aims of the work and also instruct them in the means and methods of achieving those aims. However, this is not necessarily so. If we specify particular means and methods for achieving the aims of the work and compel people to follow them, the people receiving these instructions often will not think seriously about the aims of the work even though they have been told about them. Moreover, if the aims are not achieved, people may try to evade responsibility by claiming that they have been told to use unsuitable means and methods.

When it is easy for people to make excuses, their sense of responsibility toward the work tends to evaporate. Also, people become intent on finding excuses for avoiding responsibility when the work goes badly, rather than trying by hook or by crook to achieve the objectives of the job they have been assigned. Clearly the aims of the work will not be achieved.

Preparing for failure by searching for pretexts to evade responsibility requires a good deal of creative energy. However, as long as creative energy is being generated, it would be much better to use it to achieve the aims of the work, from the point of view of mental health as much as from anything else.

The sense of responsibility toward work which we are talking about here is not the after-the-fact type of responsibility involved in writing explanations or apologies, but the before-the-fact type of responsibility which we could define as a strong desire to achieve, by some means or other, the aims of the assigned work.

Creativity—Mandatory Objectives, Optional Methods

For a person to experience an almost painful degree of

responsibility toward his or her work and to achieve the objectives of that work, the following two conditions must be fulfilled:

1) The objectives of the work must be clear.
2) There must be as great a degree of freedom as possible in the means and methods by which the objectives can be achieved.

As the previous example of the machine-centered approach shows, a strong sense of responsibility cannot be expected to arise if people are not told the true objectives of their work but are only given detailed instructions concerning specific means and methods to be used and are forced to follow them. Even if the objectives of the work are made clear, specifying particular means and methods of achieving them and demanding that they be followed only encourages people to use this as an excuse if they fail to achieve the objectives.

If the first of the above conditions (clarification of the true objectives of the work) is satisfied, people's sense of responsibility toward their work will become stronger the more freedom they have in the means and methods they can use; there is in fact a positive correlation between the two.

Given these conditions, people doing a job will often display great positivity and initiative. As noted in the previous chapter, utilizing people's creativity in their work is indispensable for motivation.

What we have been discussing so far in this chapter could be described as the "mandatory objectives, optional methods" standpoint. It is vital for creating a sense of responsibility and achieving the aims of the work.

The Goal of Work—A Healthy Company

Let us stop here to consider what we mean by work aims or objectives. The goal of a company is frequently said to be the pursuit of profit. It is certainly true that, since a company cannot be allowed to operate continually in the deficit, it must in this sense secure a profit. However, looking at this from the "mandatory objectives, optional methods" standpoint, what kind of means and methods may a company use in order to pursue profit?

What we were talking about above was not affording people complete freedom in means and methods, but giving them as much freedom as possible. Naturally, there are many necessary restrictions, legal and ethical ones being particularly important.

Further, Okusa cites the following quotation by the Spanish philosopher Ortega: "A human being has no pleasure in

[49]

simply being in the world. He takes pleasure in being good."
If we replace the words "human being" in this quotation with
"company," it tells us that a company which simply "is" in
the world has no grounds for its existence and can only wither
away; whereas a company which "is good" in the world can,
through a unique form of existence which it alone can create, be of service to the world in some form or another, and
this is vital for keeping the company alive.

Profit is both the means by which a company continues
to exist and grow and the result of this process; but simply
pursuing profit is not a company's goal.

As will be discussed further in Chapter 11, the involvement of a company's employees often increases as their
educational level rises. Industrial democracy in Northern Eu-
ropean nations and workplace QC circle activities in Japan
and other countries are outstanding examples of this. The
recent popularity of CI (corporate identity) campaigns is also
closely related.

Work objectives should be acceptable to all involved. For
this to be so, people's duties must be made clear, and they
must be fair and above-board. In expressing them verbally,
it is effective to use key words such as "appealing," "attrac-
tive," and "adventurous."

This approach will become increasingly important in the
future.

7. Creativity and Standardization

Up till now, I have been discussing the relation between the work we do and humanity, and the creativity and sociality which constitute humanity. As readers will have already realized, the motivation to work is closely related to creativity and is, in fact, inseparable from it.

Creativity and Standardization

The necessity and importance of formulating and controlling various standards for the performance of work, i.e., standardization, are often emphasized from the standpoint of improving work efficiency and assuring quality. Standardization can be broadly divided into standardization of things and standardization of work. Everybody accepts that standardizing things in various ways is indispensable, not only for simplifying after-sales service, but also for guaranteeing quality and reliability, reducing costs and improving productivity. However, as far as the standardization of work is concerned, several problems come to mind.

The first objection is that standardizing work is inconsistent with motivation, since it restricts the scope for creativity and ingenuity on the part of the people engaged in the work.

As explained in the previous chapter, we should try and allow people as much freedom as possible in the means and

methods they use in performing their work, and the more freedom we give them, the greater their sense of responsibility becomes and the more creativity they display. Does work standardization really prevent this?

The second objection is that, even after a lot of time and effort has been put into standardizing work methods, the standards are often not adhered to. For example, a survey by the Japanese Ministry of International Trade and Industry's Industrial Science and Technology Agency reported that, although most Japanese companies have regulations stipulating that their in-house standards are to be obeyed, approximately 50% of them do not have any definite procedures for ensuring that these regulations are enforced.

Preparing standards takes time and effort, and is quite a difficult job. What becomes of the efforts of those who create the standards if they are not routinely followed? Is it so difficult for workers in the workplace to follow the standards that have been set?

Creativity and Standardization

To make our discussion more concrete, let us consider the example of work standards in a production process.

Work Standards

Work standards may be set out in various ways, but they usually include the following three items:

1. The objectives of the work: taking a production process as an example, this includes the quality specifications or quality standards for the intermediate or final products which must be made in the process.
2. Constraints on carrying out the work: these consist of restrictions which must be adhered to in performing the work; items which ensure the safety of employees or assure product quality are the most important of these.
3. The means and methods to be employed in performing the work.

Of these three items, item 1 must always be achieved and item 2 must be scrupulously obeyed whoever is responsible for doing the work. In other words, everyone must make conforming products and everyone must work safely. Also, it is obvious that the fewer the restrictions listed under item 2, the greater the degree of freedom in performing the work and the easier it is to do it. Therefore, we should consider these conditions very carefully and strive to eliminate as many of them as possible.

Work standards for dangerous work are generally obeyed more scrupulously than those for other types of work, not only because dangerous work is supervised more carefully, but also because everyone is most concerned about his or her own safety.

[53]

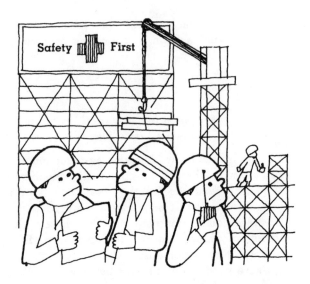

Must Means and Methods Be Obeyed?

But what about item 3? Must standardized means and methods be followed in the same way as the conditions of item 2 whoever is doing the work? As discussed in the previous chapter, setting prescribed means and methods and forcing people to obey them makes it easy for them to avoid responsibility for failure; they can claim that it was not their fault because they followed the stipulated methods. This must be strenuously guarded against.

We also tend to believe that standardized means and methods formulated after careful consideration of all the angles must be the most productive and efficient whoever is using them, and that this is why everyone must obey them —at least, the people who draw up the standards think so.

However, it is doubtful that any single standard can be the most efficient for all people considering their different characteristics and habits.

Clearly this kind of standardization of action is missing from sports. If such optimally efficient standards for action did exist in sports, anybody would be able to produce a world record by following the standards and there would be no need to hold the Olympics. To improve at a sport, we must first master the basic motions by reading books or taking lessons—but this alone will not allow us to produce a world record. To keep improving our personal best, there is no way other than to build on these basic actions through hard work—by continually practicing and exerting great ingenuity to discover the method which suits us best.

Two Types of Work Standard

Looked at from this perspective, item 3 (work standards relating to means and methods) should be divided into two types: one would consist of training manuals for beginners, equivalent to the basic motions in sports discussed above, while the other would be work standards describing methods and techniques for experienced workers. The two types should not be confused. These two types of standards must be regarded not as instructions that must be obeyed without fail, but as useful hints for carrying out the work.

The first of these two (manuals for novices) is for helping workers understand the basic actions and raising the efficiency of training while they are learning the job. The manuals should be written as simply and clearly as possible.

It is also important to make it clear to all trainees at the end of their basic training that the working methods they have learned so far are no more than basic actions, and that, hav-

ing mastered them, they should try to develop methods that suit their own individual physiques and temperaments. They should be told that this will help them to improve their skills, and that their company actively supports and encourages them in doing so. Conversely, forcing novices to perform basic actions exactly as they have been taught not only leads to shirking of responsibility but also prevents them from improving their skills. Such an approach is nothing short of ridiculous.

When workers' skills improve and they use their own initiative to develop the basic actions into practical working methods, these can be included in the work standards for experienced workers. There should be a system for recording the hints and tips brought up by individuals or groups, and this should be actively encouraged. At the same time, guidance should be given to ensure that the procedures do not contravene any of the restrictions of item 2 and that correct working methods are proposed and recorded.

Since it will be possible to incorporate most of the work methods recorded in this way into the basic actions, the basic actions themselves should also be revised periodically, further increasing their effectiveness.

Creativity and standardization are not mutually exclusive but, on the contrary, mutually complementary. Through this kind of standardization, people actually engaged in the work can make full use of their creativity, discover methods of doing the work even better, and make efforts to enhance and improve item 3. Again, since we can expect workers' own skills to improve as a result, it should not be left entirely up to them. Managers and staff should offer as much encouragement and assistance as possible.

8. Breakthrough

Creativity is one of the indispensable elements of motivation. This chapter considers it further from the viewpoint of breaking out of the status quo.

Let us take the production process as an example. The most important objective of production is to make products of a quality which matches the quality of design expressed in quality specifications and standards. In other words, it is to manufacture conforming products. Producing products of conforming quality, i.e., good products, is more important even than reducing costs or increasing productivity. There is no point in increasing productivity if we are turning out nonconforming products.

Production Cost and Defect Rate—Optimization or Breakthrough?

On the other side of the coin, the deep-rooted idea exists that we should try to achieve an optimum value of the defect rate in relation to the production cost. Let me start by explaining what this idea entails.

The production cost of a manufactured article generally consists of the following three items:

1) Basic production cost: the expenditure needed for production, such as personnel costs, equipment depre-

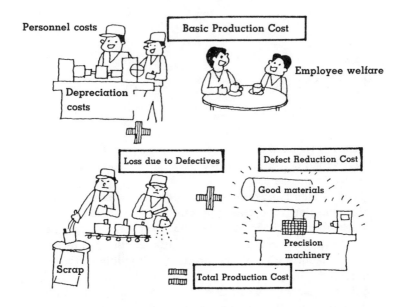

ciation costs, employee welfare costs, etc. These are regarded as constant whether the defect rate is high or low.

2) Losses due to defects: the costs associated with producing nonconforming products and the accompanying scrap and rework, including the costs of dealing with complaints and doing repair work under guarantee. We should take a stern approach in defining these costs, including in them items such as the value of the good products which could have been made with the man-hours spent on reworking defective products.

3) Defect reduction costs: the cost incurred in reducing the defect rate. It is not very high when the defect rate is high, but increases rapidly when the defect rate drops, because it then becomes necessary to purchase

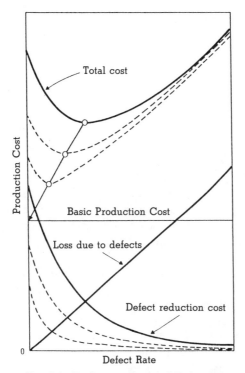

Fig. 1.3 **Production Cost and Defect Rate**

precision machinery, to use better-quality materials, etc.

According to the above assertion and as the solid lines in Fig. 1.3 show, the losses due to defects in a production process decrease approximately in proportion to a decrease in the defect rate, while the cost of reducing the defect rate increases steeply. The total production cost thus initially decreases as the defect rate decreases, but turns round and begins to increase as the defect rate approaches zero, as shown in the figure. For this reason, an optimum defect rate exists at which the production cost is at a minimum.

However, if we examine the idea a little more closely, the following doubts appear.

The first is that the value of the defect rate at which the production cost is at a minimum may indeed be the optimum value for the manufacturer, but is it really the optimum value for the customers? The most desirable thing from the customer's viewpoint is that all the products that he or she buys and uses should be defect-free. Keeping the production defect rate at this optimum value and achieving a zero defect rate in shipped products by subsequent 100% screening is not such an easy option when we consider the errors associated with 100% screening and the loss of reliability produced by reworking.

Second, except for the case in which the manufacturer has a monopoly on the market and has no competitors, competing manufacturers may find some method of both lowering the defect rate and reducing the production cost. If this happens, it is clear that the first manufacturer will lose out to the competition. Clinging to its own optimum defect rate will be of no use at all if the company is trounced by its rivals.

How have we managed to get ourselves into this odd situation? It is because the idea discussed above contains a basic inconsistency.

It is certainly true that, of the three types of costs mentioned, the basic production cost and the losses due to defects can both be calculated unambiguously provided that they have been clearly defined and a basis for their computation has been decided. They can then be shown as separate solid lines on a graph, as in Fig. 1.3. However, it is doubtful whether we can really calculate the cost of reducing the de-

fect rate unambiguously in the same way, even if we define it clearly.

We know that there are always a number of possible ways for improving the quality of a product and that there is always room for further improvement in any particular method we have thought up. In this sense, our improvement plans are never the best nor the only ones possible. In other words, the cost of reducing the defect rate shown in Fig. 1.3 is not fixed like the other two types of costs but is variable.

Let us imagine that we have refined our defect reduction plan further and have succeeded in reducing the defect rate at a cost shown by one of the broken lines in the lower half of the figure, i.e., at a lower cost than that shown by the solid line. The minimum value of the total production cost will then decrease correspondingly and the optimum value of the defect rate will also drop.

By making an even greater effort, it may be possible to lower the total production cost and the optimum value of the defect rate even further. As shown in Fig. 1.3, if we discover a method of reducing the defect rate without incurring any cost, the minimum value of the total production cost will become equal to the basic production cost at a defect rate of zero, while the optimum defect rate will be zero. This is our ultimate, ideal objective.

Some people are of the opinion that reducing the defect rate to zero at zero cost is no more than an impossible dream and that trying to do so is simply building castles in the air. It would certainly be foolish to waste energy attempting to achieve this goal if it had been proven impossible. However, nobody can actually prove that it is incapable of attainment. Essentially, it falls into the category of those things which you never know whether you can do or not until you have tried. Surely not knowing whether or not something is possible until we have tried it makes it all the more worthwhile taking a shot at it.

Also, setting up an ultimate objective is a valuable way of directing our energies.

Preconditions for Breakthrough

The above approach to problem solving leads to creative breakthroughs and is radically different from superficial optimization based on the idea of preserving the status quo. There are always many different ways of reducing defects, and this is why the cost of doing so is not fixed but variable. In turn, the minimum value of the production cost and the defect rate which corresponds to it are also variable, and this is the basis for the breakthrough attitude.

A further stimulus for making this kind of breakthrough

was the quality-cost dilemma, by which costs increase as the defect rate is lowered. To solve this problem, we had to find ways of lowering costs while at the same time improving quality, and this required limitless creativity on our behalf.

Other similar dilemmas, e.g., that between productivity and quality or that between employee safety and productivity demand our attention. The willpower and tenacity necessary to solve these problems are the source of our creativity and lead to breakthroughs.

The following words of Dr. Deming concerning productivity and quality are particularly interesting in this regard: "Productivity goes up as quality goes up. This fact is well known, but only to a select few."

If we compare the creative, breakthrough type of approach with the optimizing, status-quo-preserving type of approach, we see that the latter is usually logical and easily accepted, while the former tends to be more emotional than logical, is generally difficult for people to accept readily, and is easily overruled. What basically supports it is the strong determination and tenacity of purpose of those advocating it. In addition, the full understanding and whole-hearted support of superiors and others concerned will provide a strong backing for it.

Four Steps for Making Work More Creative

Making work more creative is important for motivation. The steps required to effect such changes have been mentioned sporadically throughout these pages, and I would like to summarize them here.

(1) When giving work instructions, clarify the true aims of the work.

Part 1: WHAT IS MOTIVATION?

This was discussed in Chapter 6. Instead of explaining clearly what the aim of a job is, we tend to concentrate on the methods and means to be used for achieving that aim. However, every job has an aim, and it goes without saying that achieving this aim is the most important thing.

In the extreme case, there is no need to use the specified means and methods as long as the stated objective is achieved. Aside from mandatory restrictions relating to safety and quality assurance, information concerning means and methods should be given for reference only, and we should encourage people to devise their own best ways of achieving the objectives.

(2) See that people have a strong sense of responsibility toward their work.

This is related to (1) above. As noted in Chapters 6 and 7, human beings are often weak and irrational and tend to try to shift responsibility onto someone else when their work goes badly, complaining or being evasive. It is therefore necessary to devise ways of nipping such excuses in the bud whenever they seem likely to appear.

The "mandatory objectives, optional means" approach described in (1) above serves this purpose, and techniques such as the stratification of data, the correction of data by mean value or by regression, and the application of the orthogonal principle in the design of experiments are all effective devices for putting a stop to excuses.

(3) Give time for the creation of ideas.

If steps (1) and (2) are followed, people will feel a keen sense of responsibility for solving their problems come what may. When they feel such a strong sense of responsibility, they will go back to the essence of the problem and think about it deeply, and this will result in flashes of inspiration and the creation of new ideas. Excellent ideas are most easily generated during those times when we have pondered the problem deeply and have arrived at a detached, meditative state of mind.

An ancient Chinese proverb tells us that this kind of time occurs when we are horseback riding, lying down and relaxing, or sitting on the toilet. The times at which ideas come most readily are different for every individual. The important thing is to give people the time to be creative.

(4) Nurture ideas and bring them to fruition.

Newborn ideas created in this way are extremely fragile. If they are examined critically with the idea of picking them to pieces or squashing them down, it is very easy to obliterate them completely. However, to find out whether such ideas are really good or not, or to develop them in superior ways, they must be allowed to grow. There is no objection during

this stage of growth to allowing an idea to change gradually from its original form into a better one.

It is often said that the main enemies of new product development are to be found within the company itself. This means that more people are concerned with going around stepping on new ideas than with encouraging their development. A new idea is like a newborn baby, and raising it to maturity always requires someone to look after its interests and act as a loving parent. In most cases, those in positions of authority are the only ones who can play this role.

In other words, managers should not go around throwing cold water on new ideas but should become their patrons and encourage their growth.

Only by passing through steps (1) to (4) will it be possible for work to be reborn as a creative activity. If ideas are created and fostered, those concerned will come to feel a real sense of self-confidence. This is an extremely valuable experience from the standpoint of motivation, and is nothing less than the positive feedback shown by the arrows in Fig. 1.2.

9. Learning From Results

Defects and Abnormalities

The plan-do-check-act series of activities aimed at creating an upward improvement spiral, first proposed by Dr. Deming and subsequently dubbed the "PDCA cycle" has, in conjunction with quality control activities, been widely adopted both in Japan and abroad. The particular activities that exhibit the features of statistical quality control lie in the "check"

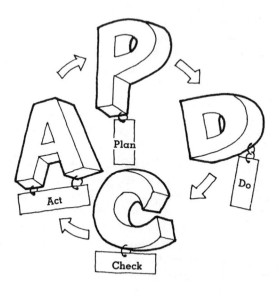

and "act" phases. These consist of detecting abnormalities in the results of work, investigating and identifying their causes, and taking corrective action. Such action can be of the following two types:

1) Adjustments designed to correct deviations from the standard value (stopgap measures).
2) Prevention of recurrence in which a statistical abnormality is detected, its cause is investigated and identified, and the process is improved (permanent measures).

Since the first type of action consists of correcting a symptom rather than a cause, it does not require the cause to be understood. Emphasis is placed on rework, and nothing is done to alter the probability of the same problem recurring in the future.

In contrast to this, the second type of action tries to prevent any recurrence by investigating the underlying causes of the abnormality and improving the process on the basis of the information gained. Even if each individual improvement is slight in itself, there will be a gradual overall improvement in the work as a result of the accumulation of many such improvements. Japanese-style quality control therefore stresses the importance of the second type of action, i.e., permanent, lasting measures as opposed to temporary, stopgap measures.

If we replace the words "standard value" in 1) above with "quality specification," 1) is equivalent to inspection and reworking of rejected products, while 2) corresponds to process control using control charts. This is straying somewhat from the subject of this book, but the two most important points in the quality assurance of manufacturing processes are not to produce defective products and not to allow abnormalities to occur. Again, the former corresponds to 1) while the latter corresponds to 2). In order not to produce defective products, the process capability index must be 1.33 or greater, while the prevention of abnormalities requires the process to remain in a state of control as indicated by properly drawn-up control charts.

Since these two conditions are more or less independent of each other, we cannot feel secure about the quality assurance of a process merely because the process capability index is 1.33 or greater or the control charts show a state of control. Both these conditions must be satisfied at the same time.

Praise and Blame

The permanent measures discussed above are of course an important type of action, but further reflection on the way we generally do things shows that we tend to concentrate our corrective actions exclusively on examining results to detect unusually bad ones, then checking their causes and eliminating them. Shortcomings and flaws tend to catch the eye more readily than good results and are therefore easier to spot. However, does simply picking out weak points and correcting them lead to real improvement?

As we well know, for every shortcoming there will be some advantage hiding in the background. But, while defects and faults stand out, merits and strong points are often difficult to spot. Actively trying to pick out these hard-to-find good points and not begrudging the effort required to make the most of them are a vital part of permanent and lasting action.

This is particularly important when dealing with people. If we pick on the weak points in a person's idea and declare it no good, the person will lose heart and the idea will not be developed and brought to fruition. However, if we find

the good points and commend the person for them, he or she will feel pleased that we have accepted the idea, and the person doing the praising will feel it necessary to do something more than just praise. Such feelings form the soil in which ideas can flourish.

Seize opportunities for teaching people. These opportunities occur when people have made mistakes that they regret and want to correct, or when they feel happy because they have just been praised. When such chances arise, be generous in overlooking mistakes and employ humor and encouragement.

A Critique of Management by Objectives

Some people advocate the use of the method known as management by objectives, which originated in America. First a topic is selected, and individual employees or groups of employees then set themselves improvement targets connected with this topic and try to achieve the targets. The results obtained are evaluated in terms of how close they get to the set targets.

If the targets are mandatory ones handed out by the higher echelons of management, employees are liable to try to find plausible excuses if the targets are not met. Even when the employees themselves set the targets, when the results are evaluated in terms of how close they approach the targets, setting a low expectation means that little effort is needed to achieve the goal and to obtain a good evaluation. As a result, this method tends to encourage people to withhold their effort,—a strange and undesirable situation.

To ensure that this kind of thing does not happen, it is best not to evaluate results in terms of their closeness to the targets. It is good to have people set their own targets, but the evaluation of their efforts should not depend on these. Instead, it is better to give a higher priority to evaluating people's efforts by means of control charts.

Fig. 1.4 is an example of a control chart for percent defective. In this chart, a run of 10 points can be seen below the central line starting on 28 November, showing that the defect rate is abnormally low for this period. This abnormality would be obvious even if the defect rate had not reached the self-set target during the period.

It is well known that abnormalities in control charts show that a change has occurred in the population, or process, with a probability of making an error of the first kind (concluding that a shift has occurred in a population parameter when in fact none has) of approximately 0.3%. Identifying the cause of the abnormality shown in the figure, i.e., finding out why the process has clearly changed for the better, is important in that it leads to permanent improvement.

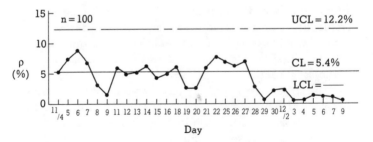

Fig. 1.4 Example of ρ-Chart

In this example, the cause of the abnormality might be unusual exertion on the part of employees, or it might be that, through their own creativity and ingenuity, they have discovered a new method. It is important not to concern ourselves solely with whether the results obtained meet the targets, but to find out why and in what ways the process has changed. This will tell us what kind of efforts the people working on the process have made and what kinds of creativity and ingenuity they have exercised.

Appropriate recognition of this kind of effort is extremely important for motivating people. Even if the results still fall short of the targets, we should be sure to recognize and encourage improvement. If we do so, the results will eventually surpass the targets and go on improving rapidly.

10. Teamwork

Teamwork From the Outside

As discussed in Chapter 6, when giving out job instructions, it is vital to state the real objectives of the work clearly at the same time as allowing as much freedom as possible in the means and methods employed to achieve those objectives. This will make the people responsible for performing the work feel a keen sense of responsibility toward it.

The aims of the work must be fully accepted by those charged with carrying out the job. To achieve this, managers and supervisors must exercise all their efforts of persuasion. We should avoid forcing people to do a job by simply saying that "orders are orders."

However, it is rare for any job done in a company to be completely self-contained and totally independent of any other work going on in the organization. Normally the various jobs distributed among individuals or groups are connected with each other in one way or another. Even if jobs appear at first glance to be unrelated, examining them by actively using the customer-oriented approach will often show a connection.

In order to achieve the true objectives, all individuals and groups must feel a deep sense of responsibility in tackling the particular jobs which they have been assigned. At the same time, however, it is important that they maintain a strong interest in other work related to their own.

Part 1: WHAT IS MOTIVATION?

For example, let us consider the work of design and manufacture. As is often explained in descriptions of quality assurance activities, we start by creating the quality of design of a product at the design stage with the aim of obtaining customer satisfaction and achieving fitness for use in the expected environment. At the subsequent production stage, we create the product quality which conforms to the quality of design and obtain customer satisfaction by providing this quality. This is the general outline of quality assurance.

If the quality of design created in this way were perfect and a product with exactly that quality were manufactured, we would have achieved the ultimate in quality assurance. In such a case, all the production department would have to do would be to follow the design. However, it is unlikely that a quality of design devised by a human being could ever be perfect and thus incapable of any further improvement.

This brings us to the idea of obtaining information feedback from the customer and utilizing it to improve our designs, which in turn requires teamwork among the sales, design, and production divisions.

Production follows design. If the customer-oriented approach is applied within a company, while the design division must ensure that it satisfies the product's end user, it must also try to satisfy the production division, i.e., the next process. To do this, the production division must provide the design division with information feedback, e.g., on the process capability index obtained in the production process. Doing so builds the kind of teamwork between design and production needed for improving product quality even further.

The starting point for teamwork is to have not only a keen sense of responsibility toward one's own work in order to achieve its objectives but also a strong interest in other work related to one's own. This will enable everyone to achieve their common objective.

Wonderful ideas often are generated when people with different standpoints and approaches have a strong common interest in a certain job and come together for discussion. This kind of effect is illustrated in the saying "Okame hachimoku" ("The onlookers see better than the players"). This proverb from the Japanese game of Go reminds us that people watching from the sidelines often have a more objective view than the players themselves, seeing as many as eight moves ahead and spotting some skillful moves missed by the players themselves. Conversely, no matter how many people gather together, the "two heads are better than one" effect will not be achieved if they all think along the same lines.

The above considerations are closely related to the way work is apportioned and managed on a day-to-day basis. It is important to divide the work vertically into a series of jobs in line with the work flow and to put people in charge of each job, allocating responsibility for as wide a range of work as possible commensurate with individual abilities. As discussed in Chapter 6, the true aims of the work should be made perfectly clear to the people to whom it has been distributed, and they should be made to feel a strong sense of responsibility for it.

Reaching Out

It is also advisable not to draw clear lines of demarcation between jobs, but to widen people's range of responsibilities so that they overlap and create common interests with others in related work areas. The resulting "reaching out" is good for teamwork.

When work is allocated in this way, people's abilities should be judged in terms of the range of work they take on, not in terms of the amount of responsibility they have been given. Also, enlarging the range of people's work as their skills increase not only serves as a means of recognizing their growing ability but is also an extremely useful way of motivating them.

As discussed in Chapter 1, motivation started to become a problem in Europe and America from the beginning of the 1970s. There was intense discussion of the pros and cons of the Taylor-type production-line manufacturing system and its dehumanizing effects. This type of discussion made Volvo of Sweden want to have the ideal factory of the 1990s, and the company constructed its Kalmar facility, a plant without conveyor belts. But why was there so little discussion of the production-line system in Japan?

This is just a guess on my part, but the lack of interest in this concept in Japan seems only natural. The Japanese have never embraced the Western idea of drawing up clear job demarcation lines and confining people to discharging their responsibility within strict boundaries. Instead, Japanese employees have a strong common interest in neighboring areas of work, making it easy for teamwork to flourish.

Cooperation and Competition

In the management of routine work, it is far more effective for people to recognize each other's individual characteristics and make the best possible use of them than to ignore individual differences and wipe them out by "standardizing."

[79]

Part 1: WHAT IS MOTIVATION?

Clearly indicating the true aims of the work and allowing freedom to choose the means and methods (as discussed in Chapter 6) is related to this. It is an approach that engenders cooperation among people with different temperaments and ways of doing things and encourages creativity.

The human desire for improvement is closely related to the sense of competition which social beings always have, whether actively displayed or carefully concealed. The Japanese word for "competition," "kyoso," is usually written with two characters meaning "compete" and "quarrel" respectively, but the second character can be replaced by one meaning "run" without changing the word's pronunciation. I prefer to use the latter because I would like to see competition, like a race, take place in the sportsmanlike spirit of fair play. It should also be noted that this kind of competitive spirit exists not only among rival groups but also among the members of a single group who ought to be cooperating with each other.

It is important to avoid suppressing this competitive drive, since this would hamper the desire for improvement and spirit of inquiry which are so valuable for human beings. Rather, we should concentrate on ensuring that any competition which takes place does so within the rules and does not contravene the spirit of fair play. In other words, the competition must stay within the constraints mentioned in Chapter 7 under which the work must be carried out.

If fair competition exists together with teamwork among the people responsible for different jobs, the mutual interaction of the two will enhance everyone's abilities.

11. Leadership and Participation

An Example

As our lives become more affluent and our educational levels rise, we start to exercise our individuality more. The following kinds of things tend to happen as a reflection of this social trend.

Those in positions of authority tend to discuss every trifling thing with their subordinates even though they find it annoying and time-consuming, for fear that they may be faced with opposition later on if they do not do so. Meanwhile, although they take part in the discussions, the same subordinates sit there thinking that a real leader should not have to discuss every little thing with them. As a result, both parties end up wasting their time.

We experience this kind of thing every day, and I believe it is one of the reasons why the 1970s onward have become a difficult time for managers. It makes us question what leadership and participation actually are.

However, we also know that good leadership is essential for achieving work objectives and getting results. But what is leadership? A consideration of leadership is important, but we soon see that, by itself, it is an abstract concept.

Leadership and Its Preconditions

Leadership is not a matter of simply saying, "Shut up and

follow me!" It does not consist of separating the planning and execution functions, so that leaders draw up the plans and then compel their followers to carry them out. Leadership means convincing one's subordinates to accept the group's common purpose and to go all out to achieve it. The successful leader persuades subordinates to accept objectives and to agree that they are worthwhile; displays tenacity and patience while goals are being reached; and guides, develops and encourages subordinates.

We can therefore list the following specific items as preconditions for leadership:

1) Leaders must have a "dream" (a vision, an ideal, a common purpose or an ultimate objective).
2) Leaders must have the strength of will and tenacity of purpose to do whatever is necessary to realize this "dream." Patience and perseverance are included.
3) Leaders must be able to win the support of their followers. For this to happen, the "dream" must be sufficiently worthwhile.
4) Leaders must be able to do more than their followers and must actually do so. They must not interfere with what their followers can do for themselves. They must act when their followers cannot (in other words, they must be able to lead in a crisis). They must foster capable followers.
5) Leaders must always succeed, but they must never sacrifice their followers in order to do so.
6) Leaders must give the right advice to their followers at the right times.

We may not suddenly be able to display all these preconditions for leadership. However, it is vital that we bear them in mind and make a continuous effort to attain them.

Realizing Our Dreams

Some feel that as people become more and more individual-
istic it becomes increasingly difficult to find a dream which
their followers can sympathize with and to establish it as their
group's common purpose. However, every human being has
the desire to improve; we all compare our present situation
with what it could be, and try to progress by identifying
problems and solving them.

Moreover, in a group such as a business corporation which
is oriented toward achieving specific goals, it is always possible to find a particular dream which we can persuade our
subordinates to share in if we go back to the basic philosophy
of the organization and ponder it. First of all a leader needs
the ability to convince followers of the importance of realizing the dream and to persuade them to accept it.

It is better not to start simply by holding up the final objective as the goal to be reached. A more practical method
is to set relatively easy intermediate objectives and rotate the
PDCA cycle as these are gradually attained, allowing everyone to share in the joy of achievement while they continually try to raise their abilities.

The more people suffer in the course of achieving these
objectives, the greater their joy in achieving them. In fact,
the very existence of difficulties spurs us on to exert our ingenuity in overcoming them. This kind of effort naturally
leads to the development of creativity and, in its turn, raises
our abilities.

The Steps for Raising Ability

The work of a corporation is divided and apportioned by function, by department, and to individual employees. The principle of autonomous control is for each group or individual to continuously rotate the PDCA cycle for the work which they have been put in charge of. The secret of success in this is for managers to devise and implement systems that facilitate the rotation of the PDCA cycle and to give appropriate guidance and encouragement to assist people in carrying out their daily work.

When the ability of subordinates is enhanced in this way, it is important to involve them in a wider range of work, make them see the importance of their own jobs within the larger picture, and give them a strong sense of responsibility. As mentioned in the last chapter, teamwork requires people to understand and be deeply concerned not only with their own work but also with that of their colleagues and seniors. This in turn naturally raises individual abilities even further. These steps are illustrated in Fig. 1.5.

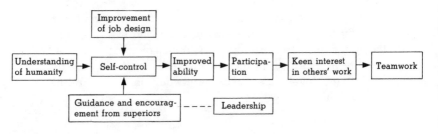

Fig. 1.5 **The Steps to Improved Ability**

The Benefits of Participation

From the preceding discussion, we can reach the following conclusion concerning participation: if it does not result in an increase in the abilities of leaders, group members, and everyone else involved, true participation has not taken place.

Real participation has the following benefits:

1) A sense of responsibility for the work is created and the PDCA cycle is rotated.
2) Intragroup communication is enhanced and interpersonal relations improve.
3) Group members' hidden talents are exercised and their human qualities utilized.
4) The group structure is transformed from a simple leader–follower arrangement to a multilevel one. This changes the group structure from a rigid and inflexible one to a flexible one capable of acting as the occasion demands. This in turn promotes reliable teamwork and the ability to respond rapidly in a crisis.
5) Group members' initiative and independence are exercised.
6) Vague goals are clarified and transformed into common objectives.
7) The division of roles for achieving the group's common objectives is clearly decided after acceptance by all the group members.
8) The number of possible ways of achieving the objectives increases, and it becomes possible to exercise the abilities of every group member.

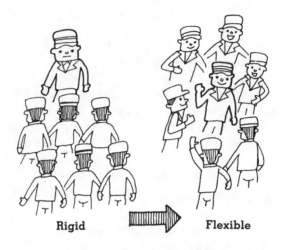

Rigid ➡️ **Flexible**

9) The leader's abilities improve and are supplemented by those of the group members.
10) All members' capabilities are broadened and enhanced.
11) Instead of group members' individuality being stifled, it is fully exercised in trying to achieve the group's common objectives.
12) Cooperation is achieved among the group members.

In listing only these good points, I fear I may have made the picture appear too rosy. However, these benefits can be used as checkpoints when reflecting on whether real participation has in fact been achieved.

Real Participation

As stated at the beginning of this chapter, participation for form's sake is sometimes used by managers as a means of self-protection. However, decisions made with this kind of participation often try to be all things to all people and are based on protecting individual interests. If managers start to use participation in this way, the participants also start trying to evade their own responsibilities. Although it can be claimed that a decision made in this way has been agreed to by everybody, the outcome is that nobody will take responsibility for it. This is the opposite of the real participation discussed above.

The timing of participation is also important. When there is a great sense of urgency and the group feels that it must rapidly break the deadlock and improve the situation, even if the problem to be tackled is not clearly defined, participation produces the best and most unexpected results. The true benefits of participation cannot be expected without such a sense of urgency.

Some people feel that, even though involving people in this way may be an effective method, having a group's members participate in every plan will undermine the authority of the leader. From one viewpoint, this opinion is correct. As mentioned earlier in relation to the prerequisites for leadership, a person who does not have a constant dream (i.e., common objective) is not qualified to be a leader, even though this dream may be modified slightly by the participation of group members. And, participation without leadership tends to produce the protectionist, please-all type of decision.

Is it all right for a leader to force his dream willy-nilly on the members of his group? In certain situations, it can be both necessary and effective. However, it is limited to the kind of situation in which there is a wide difference in the abilities of the leader and subordinates, or when the leader and the group members are thinking along very different lines. The necessity for it will probably disappear as the abil-

ities of the group members improve as a result of participation.

When people are involved in decision making, they feel
happy when their opinions are taken up, debated, and actually implemented. Thus, at the same time as using powers
of persuasion to convince the group members to accept the
dream, the leader must be prepared to listen with an open
mind to their opinions. It is this kind of discussion which
brings out the group's creativity.

Some people think that this type of participation is too
time-consuming and tedious. It is true that involving and per-
suading a large number of people is a job that takes time.
However, if this participation raises the abilities of all the
members of the group, the time needed to reach decisions
will be reduced and immeasurable benefits will be attained
through improvement in the quality of participation.

12. Summary

Human Motivation

Stimulating people's desire to work, i.e., human motivation, has been regarded as important since ancient times. I believe it will become even more important in the future as our educational standards rise and our lives become more affluent.

We are well aware of the importance of human motivation—but how can we motivate people in practice? Since motivation is a matter of moving people's hearts and minds, it is not a question of technical know-how and is therefore probably not amenable to standardization.

In discussing human motivation, we often tend to dwell on differences, e.g., the differences between Japanese and American culture or the different psychological makeup of individuals. Such considerations may be interesting from the standpoint of investigating culture or human nature, but they are not of much practical use in actually motivating people.

Chapter 1 tells us not to pursue these differences but to search out the common elements, i.e., the greatest common divisor, of human motivation. As we have seen, there is a surprisingly large amount of common ground. We do not work merely to earn money. There is something apart from money which brings us running toward rewarding work. Identifying this "Ingredient X" is the central theme in any investigation of human motivation.

Providing Satisfiers

Our discussion started by comparing Maslow's hierarchy of human needs and Herzberg's motivation theory. According to Maslow, human beings always have a variety of different needs, and their relative importance changes as people become better-off. These differing needs correspond to Herzberg's satisfiers and dissatisfiers, and it is clear that to motivate people we must not only try to remove sources of dissatisfaction, but also take positive steps to provide sources of satisfaction. These satisfiers correspond to the "Ingredient X" (something other than money) mentioned above.

Such considerations of human motivation include the content of work itself, the way in which it is apportioned, and what significance it holds for us. Providing satisfiers (Ingredient X) is made more difficult or easy by the nature of the work and the way in which it is allocated.

The Three Elements of Work

Nishibori's and O'Toole's ideas about human work (discussed in Chapter 3) are extremely valuable in this connection. Although the two men conducted their research independently, their results fit together. Both of them cite creativity, physical activity, and sociality as the indispensable elements constituting work. In addition to physical activity, which could also be described as the joy of physical exertion, it is vital to incorporate the elements of creativity (the joy of thinking) and sociality (the joy of sharing pleasure) into our work and to improve the work itself so that it is easier to incorporate these elements.

When we were poor, work and money were closely linked. There was a clear distinction between work and leisure: work is for earning money, leisure uses it up. Now that we are better-off, the distinction between work and leisure has become blurred. The steady increase in the type of work that cannot be clearly distinguished from leisure is a feature of modern society.

Humanity and the Fun of Sports

Everybody enjoys leisure activities. A typical leisure activity is sports, and, in Chapter 4, I tried to analyze those elements that make sports fun and investigate whether they

Part 1: WHAT IS MOTIVATION?

could be applied to work. At first glance, work and leisure appear to be mutually exclusive activities, but I believe that there are close similarities between the two, and that it is important for human motivation to make use of these similarities.

If we probe deeper into the origins of the pleasure to be found in sports, we arrive at an underlying base which we could term humanity. Sports are fun because they fulfill our human needs. As discussed in Chapter 5, it is very difficult for us to understand the concept of humanity if we adopt the metaphysical approach used in philosophy and psychology.

However, if we adopt the approach of cerebral physiology and define humanity as those qualities displayed by humans and not by other animals as a result of the different functioning of the human brain, it becomes much easier to understand.

Creativity and sociality can be cited as the two main elements constituting humanity, and this is closely related to the three elements of work mentioned above. Therefore, it is important in human motivation to build humanity into our work and to exercise it fully.

Functions such as creativity and sociality are frequently seen in higher-order animals, not only in humans, but there is a big difference in the degree to which they are apparent. Also, we must bear in mind that the structure and function of the human brain are exactly the same for all human beings regardless of their skin color or racial origin.

As I have repeatedly emphasized, the secret of human motivation is to actively incorporate humanity into our work and exercise it fully. So, what is the best way of going about this? In our discussion, we have concentrated on creativity as one of the most important elements of humanity.

A Sense of Responsibility

As discussed in Chapter 2, the content of work and the way in which work is allocated both affect human motivation. Chapter 6 discusses the best way of giving people a strong sense of responsibility toward their work. When talking about responsibility, we mean the strong feeling that one must somehow or other achieve the objectives of a job which one has been given.

Provided the aims of the work have been clearly explained, people's sense of responsibility will increase in proportion to the freedom they are allowed in the means and methods by which they can achieve those aims.

In performing any job, we do need certain restrictions for ensuring safety and securing quality, but we should try to keep these to a minimum. People will naturally exercise their creativity and ingenuity if allowed wide leeway in means and methods.

The Ends and Means of Work

The ends of work means objectives that are fair and above-
board, in which everyone's duties are clear and with which
everyone can agree and sympathize. Quality is one objective capable of fulfilling these conditions.

In discussing creativity the objection often arises that
creativity is inconsistent with standardization. According to
this contention, the scope for creativity becomes narrower
as work is standardized, and it is eventually snuffed out al-
together.

As discussed in Chapter 7, work standards consist of a
description of the aims of the work which must be achieved

whoever is in charge of the job (e.g., quality standards), constraints which everyone must obey in order to ensure safety or maintain the quality built in by the previous processes, and a description of the means and methods to be used for attaining the objectives of the work. Of these, the description of the means and methods is essentially different from the other two items; it should be regarded not as orders to be obeyed by everyone, come what may, but as important information for reference to be used when needed.

In other words, it is vital for everyone to treat these means and methods as "basic actions" and try to build on them to create even better and more appropriate "applied actions." This, too, will create a sense of responsibility and release vast stores of originality and ingenuity.

Creativity

Some people claim that there is always a trade-off between factors such as quality and cost and quality and productivity and that improving one will adversely affect the other. They say that making the quality of a product or service too good will have the undesired effect of raising costs and lowering productivity and that quality improvement should, like all things, be taken in moderation. However, this attitude ignores the desires of the customer who actually uses the product, and it also suffers from complacency in that it disregards the existence of competitors.

As discussed in Chapter 8, the flaw in this argument is that it overlooks the multiplicity of quality improvement methods possible. It regards the optimum value of quality as being fixed, whereas it is in fact variable. When we realize this, we can exercise our creativity to find better methods for improving quality. If we then adopt these methods,

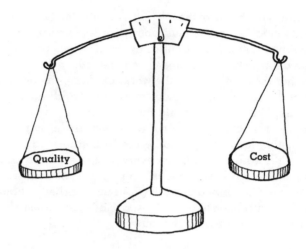

improved quality results in both lower costs and higher productivity.

Achieving such breakthroughs is made possible only by the determination of all those involved to make radical improvements by whatever means necessary, together with the wholehearted support and understanding of their bosses.

These considerations are summarized at the end of Chapter 8 in the form of the four steps required to achieve creativity.

Teamwork, Leadership, and Participation

Chapters 9 through 11 summarize the factors which those in positions of authority should consider in connection with human motivation.

The type of teamwork discussed in Chapter 10, a particularly Japanese trait not often found in other countries, will probably become even more important for Japanese companies in the future as they encounter more and more opportunities to expand abroad. The employee participation discussed in Chapter 11 and the type of leadership which is aware of this will also become more important all over the world.

Conclusion

To conclude Part 1 of this book, I would like to quote a short poem.

> "Let's get rid of management."
> People don't want to be managed,
> They want to be led.
> Whoever heard of a world manager?
> World leader, yes.
> Educational leader, political leader, religious leader, scout leader, community leader, labor leader, business leader,
> They lead.
> They don't manage.
> The carrot always wins over the stick.
> Ask your horse.
> You can *lead* your horse to water, but you can't *manage* him to drink.
> If you want to manage somebody, manage yourself.
> Do that well and you'll be ready to stop managing.
> And start leading.

> From "America no Kokoro," reproduced by kind permission of Gakuseisha.

Part 2

MOTIVATION IN INDUSTRY

Case Study 1

Greater Motivation Through a Revitalized Suggestion Scheme

The History of Our Suggestion Scheme

Washino Machine Company Limited, a manufacturer of grinding machines, milling machines, lathes, presses, and other precision machine tools, continues to launch high-quality products onto the market in timely fashion in response to new demands.

Washino's suggestion scheme has a long history, having been established in 1959. However, its aims were not at first clearly defined, and it was limited merely to ordering employees to "submit suggestions." A low-key affair, it produced less than 100 suggestions per year from the whole company, a ratio of less than 0.1 per employee.

In 1983, the company embarked on a wide-ranging reform of the suggestion scheme with the aim of "stimulating the originality and ingenuity of employees in order to heighten their sense of participation, improving all areas of work, and contributing to the development of the company and better employee welfare." Priority was placed on employee participation in the scheme, with the actual details of the suggestions received given secondary importance. A department store's sales are said to be proportional to the number of customers it can tempt through its doors. Taking a hint from this, we adopted the position that the same relation would hold between the number of suggestions received and the amount of money saved through improvements, and that increasing the number of suggestions would boost everyone's sense of involvement and increase the benefits proportionally.

We started the campaign with an initial target of one suggestion per employee per month, establishing "Suggestion Months" and introducing other promotional activities. For two years, the number of suggestions rose and fell, hovering around the level of 5 or 6 per person per year.

The company decided to introduce TQC in December 1985; the time was ripe for our suggestion-scheme activities to break their mold. We moved from individual suggestions to group suggestions supplied by QC circles. At the same time, we decided to set up an annual award system for recognizing and rewarding the best suggestions of the year from both individuals and QC circles. From June 1986, the company started implementing its priority policy management items and the organization was gradually improved. We now receive an average of a little under 40 suggestions per employee per year. This is certainly not a high figure compared with other companies, but the rapid increase over the last year leads me to believe that we are not far from achieving an average of 100 per person per year.

Details of the Suggestion Scheme

* Method of Submission

Suggestions are submitted by completing a suggestion form (see Table 2.1) and either placing this in a suggestion box or handing it in to one's superior, a suggestion promo-

Table 2.1 Suggestion Form

My Suggestion	Workplace	Production Technology Division	Technical Section
	Employee Code 2 5 8 7 8	Name	Naoki Kitaoka
	Name of collaborator or circle		Comet

Submission date: 25 July 1987

Receipt no: 8 7 | 6 4 1

Request for examination to:

Section Manager

Please investigate the suggestion and reply to the secretary of the submitting division within 10 days of receipt. If it is not appropriate for you to examine the suggestion, please return this form to the office.

Title of Suggestion   Doubling of heads on position sensors

Progress of Examination
- Is being/will be adopted
- Will not/cannot be adopted

September 1987
Completed/Scheduled

This suggestion will produce the following savings:

Total Savings	Cost of Execution	Net Savings
¥1,555,000		¥1,555,000

● Problems
- ☐ Known fact
- ☐ Similar suggestion exists (date:)
- ☐ Already discussed (under discussion)
- ☐ Little benefit expected
- ☐ Will increase costs
- ☐ Technically difficult
- ☐ Will decrease quality or performance
- ☐ Will reduce safety
- ☐ Difficult because of nature of equipment
- ☐ Will increase labor
- ☐ Difficult to put into effect
- ☐ Will be submitted as a request

☐ Your suggestion cannot be adopted for the above reasons. Please resubmit if the situation changes and it becomes practicable in the future.

Completed by

Present method and weak points (what is the problem?)

Machine Model   **Part No.**   **Name of part**

Position sensors (Magnescale, Nikon, Mitsutoyo, etc.) are usually provided with one scale for each head. Detecting the position of two or more units on the same axis requires the mounting of two scales, more than doubling the man-hours and cost needed for spacing, precision mounting, covers and maintenance compared with one scale.

In the retrofitting of machinery and equipment (PL102, PL107, PL-2G), it is necessary to detect the lateral position of the toolrest on the there is no room to install the second scale, and this results in cost overruns and other difficulties.

My Suggestion and Improvements (Request for Examination by

A method of sensing position using two heads fitted to one scale...

[105]

tion committee member, or the administrative office. The routes by which suggestions can be submitted have been increased to make it easier for people to offer them.

* Method of Evaluation

A suggestion must be examined and the award procedure set in motion by the 20th of the month following that in which the suggestion is received. This rule was introduced so that nobody can complain of delays in having their suggestions evaluated.

* Awards

Awards are handed out at morning divisional assemblies at the beginning of every month. Even people who have made suggestions of minor importance or ones that have been rejected are rewarded by prizes for taking part. While the good points of suggestions may be praised where appropriate, it is forbidden to criticize their shortcomings.

Mechanisms for Invigorating Suggestion Schemes

* Annual Award Scheme

The number of suggestions varied widely from month to month. To reduce this variation, a President's award scheme was introduced in 1985 for commending groups or individuals who had scored more than a certain number of points during the year. The determination was made according to set criteria such as a suggestion's effect of implementation, degree of originality, amount of research conducted, and applicability (see Tables 2.2–2.5).

Since the points scored for a suggestion depend on its contents, awards are decided according to both the number of suggestions submitted and the points obtained for their merit. In 1985, only a few individuals and circles qualified for these awards, but the number will reach double figures in 1987.

* Suggestion Month

One month in every six was designated "Suggestion Month," and this continued until the first half of 1987. During this month, the number of suggestions submitted per person is calculated for each division and the top three divisions are officially commended. Targets for number of suggestions are also set each time, and those divisions that achieve their target receive inexpensive gifts as a reward for their effort. The top division in the first half of 1987 achieved a figure of 8.6 suggestions per month per person, and the system helped to raise the overall level of suggestions.

* Inter-Section League

From June 1987, the company was divided into blocks for a league competition (places with sections of approximately equal sizes being put in the same block). Several leagues were formed, with names such as "heavy league," "light league," etc., depending on numbers, with ten teams in each league. The winners and losers of each "match" are decided each month according to the number of suggestions submitted per person by each team. The results are displayed for everyone to see (e.g., Production Technology Section—Won 7, Lost 2; Personnel Section—Won 3, Lost 6). This campaign makes use of the principle of competition (see Table 2.6).

The teams react in various ways to this scheme, saying things like, "We're sure not going to let that section beat us," or, "We have to win at least 50% of our matches."

Part 2: MOTIVATION IN INDUSTRY

Table 2.2 Suggestion Examination

Item	Weighting	Element for Evaluation	A		B	
	5	Savings in man-hours, materials etc. (Profit points)	¥40,000,000 or over 10	¥20,000,000– ¥39,999,999 9	¥10,000,000– ¥19,999,999 8	¥5,000,000– ¥9,999,999 7
	2	Other benefits (Merit points)	Outstanding benefit 10	9	Large benefit 8	7
Idea	1	Original or imitative?	Original and excellent 10	9	Original and superior or imitative but excellent 8	7
Amount of research	1	Amount of research conducted–individual or joint effort? Assess from degree of experiment, etc.	Extremely well researched 10	9	Very well researched 8	7
	1	Range of applicability	Applicable in almost all areas of work 10	9	Applicable in other divisions 8	7
Special bonus points	For particularly meritorious features other than the above					

Notes: 1. Profit points under 'effect of implementation' should be calculated according to the following formulas:

   (A) Man-hour savings.
       Reduction in man-hours (relative to latest figures) × charge/year.
   (B) Savings in materials, etc. (materials and expenses).
       Value of savings—(increase in costs where applicable)/year.
   (C) Figures for the financial term in which the suggestion was made should be used. When the savings depend on the number of machines manufactured, the numbers quoted in the profit plans should be used.

   US$1.00 is approximately equivalent to ¥130 (Dec. 1990)

* Suggestion News

Pamphlets describing QC circle activities and suggestion activities are distributed to company employees every month.

[108]

Greater Motivation Thru a Revitalized Suggestion Scheme

Criteria

C			D			
¥3,500,000– ¥4,999,999 6	¥2,000,000– ¥3,499,999 5	¥1,000,000– ¥1,999,999 4	¥600,000– ¥999,999 3	¥300,000– ¥599,999 2	¥50,000– ¥299,999 1	Under ¥50,000 0
Considerable benefit				Some benefit		
6	5	4	3	2	1	0
Original and good or imitative but superior				Good		
6	5	4	3	2	1	0
Well researched				Researched		
6	5	4	3	2	1	0
Applicable in that particular division			Applicable in that particular workplace			
6	5	4	3	2	1	0

2. Merit points under 'effect of implementation' are for evaluating items such as the following which cannot be reckoned in monetary terms like profit points.

   (A) Items relating to safety and hygiene.
   (B) Items relating to improvements in working environment.
   (C) Items relating to improvement in workplace morale.
   (D) Other items similar to the above.

3. The profit points and merit points under 'effect of implementation' should be evaluated together.

Other information under titles such as "The A–Z of Improvement Suggestions" is also distributed in order to boost suggestion activities and provide motivation.

Part 2: MOTIVATION IN INDUSTRY

Table 2.3. President's Award Criteria

Type of Award	Grade	Score	Prize
Special Award for Excellence	Special Grade Grade 1	105 points or more 95–104 points	More than ¥100,000 ¥100,000
Award for Excellence	Grade 2 Grade 3 Grade 4	85–94 points 75–84 points 65–74 points	¥50,000 ¥30,000 ¥20,000
Award for Superiority	Grade 5 Grade 6 Grade 7	55–64 points 45–54 points 35–44 points	¥10,000 ¥ 7,000 ¥ 5,000
Merit Award	Grade 8 Grade 9 Grade 10	25–34 points 15–24 points 10–14 points	¥ 3,000 ¥ 2,000 ¥ 1,000
Award for Effort		5– 9 points	¥ 500
Participation Award		0– 4 points	Small gift

US$1.00 is approximately equivalent to ¥130 (Dec. 1990)

Table 2.4. Awards for Effort and Participation

Type of Award	Score	Prize
Award for Effort, Class A	15 points or more	¥1,000
Award for Effort, Class B	5–14 points	¥ 500
Participation Award	0– 4 points	Small gift

US$1.00 is approximately equivalent to ¥130 (Dec. 1990)

Greater Motivation Thru a Revitalized Suggestion Scheme

Table 2.5. Annual Award Criteria

Type or Award	Prize	Conditions
Gold Award	Trophy plus ¥100,000	1,000 total points for year plus at least 3 Awards for Superiority or better
Silver Award	¥50,000	800 total points for year plus at least one Award for Superiority or better
Bronze Award	¥30,000	600 total points for year plus at least one Award for Superiority or better
Award for Effort, Class A	¥20,000	500 total points for year plus at least one Award for Superiority or better
Award for Effort, Class B	¥10,000	400 total points for year plus at least one Award for Superiority or better

Notes: 1) To calculate individual points from a group suggestion, multiply the score for the suggestion by 1.5 and divide by the number of people in the group.

2) For group suggestions where individual points are not to be awarded (when the group members' names are not recorded), treat the group as an individual and award the appropriate prize to the group based on the above criteria.

3) Gold, silver and bronze awards are limited to individuals who have submitted at least 3 suggestions per month, and awards for effort (classes A and B) are limited to those who have submitted 2 or more suggestions per month. In the case of groups, the minimum numbers of suggestions per month should be multiplied by the number of members in the group.

US$1.00 is approximately equivalent to ¥130 (Dec. 1990)

[111]

Benefits and Costs

Although the objective of the suggestion scheme is to increase employee involvement, it is also interesting to look at the cost benefits derived from the suggestions. The benefits obtained in the past year were as follows:

1) Number of suggestions: 33.8 per person
2) Cost benefit: ¥371,000 per person
3) Prizes: ¥12,000 per person

Future Topics

Long management experience tells us that trying to inject vitality into an organization simply by concentrating on suggestion schemes will not work.

Just as QC circle activities only come to life through the promotion of TQC, suggestion schemes cannot be expected to give substantial results unless a corporate organization that provides for total employee participation is created.

A suggestion scheme is not succeeding if people are still saying things like, "A lot of workers don't like writing," "Is it really possible to make things more efficient?" and "The prizes are pretty cheap." It is really working only when an environment has been created in which remarks such as, "I need three more suggestions to win a prize. Has anyone got any good ideas?" are made spontaneously in social situations, e.g., when workers are relaxing together.

US$1.00 is approximately equivalent to ¥130 (Dec. 1990)

Table 2.6 Inter-Section Suggestion League (Light League) (September 1987)

Section	PH	Personnel and Health 5.75	Accounting and Planning 8.33	Purchasing 3.88	Quality Assurance and TQC 4.20	Production Technology 1 6.50	Standards and Costing 2.80	CAD 2.00	Test Fabrication Management 0.67	Technology Management 2.25	Research Technology 2.67	This Month's Results	This Month's Ranking	Cumulative Results	Overall Position
Personnel and Health	5.75		x	o	o	x	o	o	o	o	o	Won 7 Lost 2	3	Won 30 Lost 46	7
Accounting and Planning	8.33	o		o	o	o	o	o	o	o	o	Won 9 Lost 0	1	Won 28 Lost 48	8
Purchasing	3.88	x	x		x	x	o	o	o	o	o	Won 5 Lost 4	5	Won 53 Lost 23	2
Quality Assurance and TQC	4.20	x	x	o		x	o	o	o	o	o	Won 6 Lost 3	4	Won 45 Lost 30	4
Production Technology 1	6.50	o	x	o	o		o	o	o	o	o	Won 8 Lost 1	2	Won 70 Lost 6	1
Standards and Costing	2.80	x	x	x	x	x		o	o	o	o	Won 4 Lost 5	6	Won 51 Lost 24	3
CAD	2.00	x	x	x	x	x	x		o	x	x	Won 1 Lost 8	9	Won 31 Lost 43	6
Test Fabrication Management	0.67	x	x	x	x	x	x	x		x	x	Won 0 Lost 9	10	Won 15 Lost 61	9
Technology Management	2.25	x	x	x	x	x	x	o	o		x	Won 2 Lost 7	8	Won 32 Lost 44	5
Research Technology	2.67	x	x	x	x	x	x	o	o	o		Won 3 Lost 6	7	Won 3 Lost 33	10

[113]

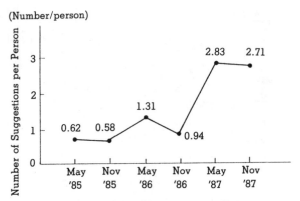

(Number/person)

Fig. 2.1   Trend in Suggestions per Person

At present, we have managed by various contrivances to increase the number of suggestions as shown in Fig. 2.1. Ideally, however, the number of suggestions submitted should increase steadily even without such devices, or with only a simple system. For this to occur, the atmosphere in the company must facilitate the implementation of suggestions. Also, everyone must understand company policy and recognize that submitting suggestions is good training for oneself, supports the company, and benefits others. Only then can a suggestion scheme be said to be truly standing on its own feet.

Case Study 2

Have People Sell a Dream

A Dream Takes Off—Encountering a Catalog

It was about two years after I transferred from my company's technical development division to my current position in the sales division that Mr. T, still recovering from a recent illness, visited me at my Osaka office.

Mr. T was on the staff of our product development laboratory, and he was trying to find new products which would support our company in the years to come. He had previously worked on solid–liquid separation technology in the area of waste water treatment, and his dream was to continue along these lines and investigate solid–liquid separation technology in the ultrafine (micron and submicron) range. He wanted to combine the results of this research with the company's existing separation technology to establish comprehensive solid-liquid separation engineering as one of our basic lines of business.

"I want to make separation technology research my mission in life," he said, handing me several sheets of data. The information he was showing me related to a bobbin-type fine filtration unit, and he had come to ask me to carry out a preliminary market survey on the device. This was the starting point of his dream, and I could not refuse his earnest request. I promised to give what little help I could.

The results of the survey, which took several weeks, were not very encouraging. Many such products were already in use, they had a limited range of applicability, and the technology was already old-hat. No great benefit could be expected from entering the market at this stage. It was therefore with a heavy heart that I prepared to send Mr. T the survey report.

It was just at this time that Mr. G, a trading company salesman, dropped in wielding a thick bundle of catalogs. "The French Embassy has been briefing us on their country's technology," he said, showing me the catalogs, which were written in French and English.

The catalog he chose to show me was about zirconia ceramic membranes for ultrafiltration and fine filtration. The features of these devices were surprising even to a layman like me. All of the membranes' characteristics, such as their applicability to a wide pH range and their high resistance to pressure, heat, and chemical corrosion, were excellent— better than any I had ever heard of before. I felt intuitively that this was what Mr. T had been looking for.

I immediately sent the materials to Mr. T and asked him for a technical evaluation. Mr. T sent back a request for a market survey together with an abridged translation of the documents. The results of the survey indicated that our customers would be happy with the characteristics of the membranes, but there was insufficient data on their actual separation performance.

Mr. T launched into an energetic investigation, and after several trips to France, we managed to forge a technical cooperation agreement with the French manufacturer. During this time, I received a steady flow of new data from Mr. T. Soon after marketing the product, we realized that it was achieving excellent results for uses such as clarifying culture solutions and removing microorganisms and proteins. Our dream grew, and we began to think that the membranes might prove to be a new weapon in the biotechnology race. Surely the technology behind them would contribute to the development of Japan's traditional fermentation technology.

Making "Real Sake"

The production of sake is a typical example of traditional Japanese fermentation technology at work. The recent boom in natural eating and health foods has also affected Japan's sake industry, and "real sake" is steadily consolidating its market share, acting as the advance guard in recovering the ground lost by sake to other alcoholic drinks.

Relying on my smattering of knowledge about real sake, I made a public relations visit at this time to the industry's biggest company, G Co., with the aim of promoting our product. Lightly brushing aside our inexpert and dressed-up attempts at a technical description, the deputy divisional manager, Mr. I, gave us the benefit of his wisdom about sake and real sake.

During the production process, refined sake undergoes two heat treatments before it is shipped as the final product. This is to deactivate the enzymes in the raw sake and kill off any bacteria, so the sake will retain its excellent flavor and bouquet for a long time. However, this pasteurizing process partially destroys the sake's mellow "nose," because much of its fragrance and flavor is furnished by low-boiling-point substances which are vaporized by heating.

Real sake, on the other hand, is given absolutely no heat treatment in order to conserve its aroma and taste perfectly. This means that it does not keep for a long time; it cannot

be distributed through the normal channels and therefore cannot be supplied to large numbers of customers.

To solve this problem, the enzymes must be eliminated from the raw sake while it is still "alive." Ultrafiltration employing functional membranes can be used to achieve this. However, the membrane must not transfer any odor to the sake, and contact with alcohol must neither make it swell nor alter its performance characteristics. Stable performance and long life are also important features.

I became keenly aware of Mr. I's uncompromising zeal in the pursuit of manufacturing real sake worthy of the name, and I felt quite humbled. As I learned more about real sake, I became confident that our ceramic membranes could be used for its production and felt a strong desire to be allowed to take part in this venture.

Mr. I was also highly interested in the results achieved with the membranes for filtering wine in France. Now it was the

[118]

turn of our technical section manager, Mr. T. Although Mr. T talked only about filtering wine, it has so much in common with the sought-after image of delicious cold "real sake" that Mr. I became more and more interested.

The Dream Is Achieved!

One of our most urgent problems was the effective operation of a trial filter unit purchased from the French company with which we had concluded the technical cooperation agreement for the zirconia ceramic membranes. Testing and evaluating this unit at G Co. would enable us to predict its future potential. We submitted a pressing request to G Co. to carry out a pilot test to provide data on which we could base our discussions about commercializing the device.

I was confident that G Co. would accept our request, but their reply was a long time in coming. A few weeks later, Mr. T ran out of patience and telephoned me. He wanted me to repeat our request to G Co. "Don't rush things, they'll soon be in touch," I said, and put the phone down. Almost at the same time, my assistant, Ms. Y, informed me that G Co. was on the line.

Restraining my eagerness, I picked up the phone. I felt that our dream and Mr. I's dream had come together. Six months later, G Co. ordered its first filtration unit from us.

Mr. T's dream was also Mr. I's dream, and it is also probably that of sake drinkers everywhere. It is a marvelous thing if, by realizing our own dreams, we can also realize those of the rest of society. This is what we want and what our companies want. It is my desire to go on being a dream-seller; as a salesman, that is my dream.

Case Study 3

Engineer Motivation—An Enthusiastic Development Team

I belong to the engineering department of a machine manufacturer and am responsible for a variety of jobs ranging from providing technical services to customers at the planning stage to the handover of the final product. We are divided into groups handling different models of machine, and I am the leader of one of these groups. There are 25 people in my group, each with different abilities and experience. I think my most important task is to motivate my group members and get them to work together so that we can exercise our full capabilities.

My View of Work as an Engineer

When I look back on 17 years with my company, I see that, at the beginning, my view of work was like the concept of subcontracting; it was something handed down from above, and I had to produce the required output by a set deadline. My motivation for working at the time was that I wanted to learn the job quickly so as to become fully competent and be accepted by those around me.

At the next stage, I was given a job in improvement and development. I investigated mechanisms that others had tried unsuccessfully to improve, and devised improvement plans incorporating the ideas of more experienced people. The results were tolerably good, and the improvements were incorporated into the designs and standardized.

Although the work went well partly because my creativity was challenged and I put a lot of effort into it, I was greatly encouraged because my superiors set appropriate objectives for me. I also received a wealth of advice from those around me, including those more experienced than myself. It was extremely rewarding to realize that my standardized improvements would be useful for designers in the future.

After two or three years, I reached the stage where I had been given a certain amount of responsibility, but I was still dealing only with people inside the company. However, when someone is given overall coordination responsibility for something, even if it is only a small project, he or she is drawn out of the company and meets people from other organizations. Even when striking up a casual conversation with someone at some meeting or other, the listener will hang on your every word when discussions turn to business. At such times, I experienced both confusion and awkwardness. However, when the work I was responsible for began to involve me directly with customers and I began to feel that I was playing an important part in providing them with the production facilities they needed, this became a strong source of motivation for me.

The Satisfaction of a Tough Fight

In most cases, our work starts with examining a customer's purchasing specifications. We interpret the customer's requirements from the text and drawings to determine the required functions and performance of the equipment, and

submit our proposal as manufacturer. The customer then checks the details of our plan to see whether or not it meets the requirements and asks us to submit a second proposal if the first is unsatisfactory. The whole process is a hard struggle in which we (the manufacturer and vendor) try to identify what will satisfy the customer and translate this into reality, while the customer (the purchaser) tries to ensure that the manufacturer will fulfill the requirements and provide satisfaction. Each side states their opinions clearly to one another and each has to approve the final result.

When one is engaged in this kind of give-and-take, the customer often comes to mind while one is working, making it impossible to do sloppy or slipshod work. One also begins to think not just about one's own job of design but also about the subsequent processes. Even without instructions from superiors, one begins to concentrate on the overall picture, considering such things as whether the deadline will be met and whether the quality assurance system is in place.

Both we and our customer continue the battle as we move through the stages of installing the equipment and doing test runs and final inspection. When the equipment performs according to the specifications, we feel pride in our work and are praised by our customer. Both of us share the resulting feeling of satisfaction. Working in earnest like this is rewarding and gives one a great sense of eagerness to get on with the next job.

Being in charge of a large project leads one to look on a completed plant as a society of human beings. One gives priority to ensuring that the equipment is easy to use, reliable, and easily maintained, so that the workers are happy to work there.

With this kind of work, one continues to be involved over a long period and encounters various difficulties along the way. However, the fact that one's work is contributing to society through the customer, and the pleasure that everyone feels when it is completed, provide a continual source of motivation and maintain one's will to work at a high level. Such experiences have led me to believe that, of the three elements of work described by Dr. Nishibori, the third (sociality or the sharing of satisfaction) is the most important as far as motivation is concerned.

Nevertheless, there are many different types of people, and there are some who will not be motivated if this "sociality" is suddenly forced on them. The way in which highly creative individuals tackle their work will change if they are given a development topic and allowed the freedom to express their own ideas. It is important to recognize that work motivation depends on the individual in this way.

An Enthusiastic Development Team

I would like now to describe a case study in which the development team in our group, although they had a hard time of it, joined forces to transform a new product which was not moving at all into a hot-selling item.

Even though we ourselves had developed and launched this product, we were always beaten by our competitors and kept on missing our chances. As a result, dissatisfaction had built up in both the technical and sales departments, and we were busy blaming each other for the mess.

As part of our sales activities, we carried out a detailed analysis of what our customers were saying and presented the product's technical weaknesses to everyone in the form of numerical data. Since the three members of the development team appeared unable to agree with this, we explained the data to them several times until they accepted it.

We then prepared a technical improvement plan and obtained everyone's assent to it, right up to the head of the operations division. We made the importance of what we were about to do very clear, informing people that everyone, including the division manager and top management, were watching closely to see what would happen. We then took the work of the three development team members, which previously they had been performing as a group, and divided it up, giving each person a clearly defined role. When this was done, the two younger members of the group came up with their own proposals and took responsibility for them. As a result, the work done by the development team improved steadily.

When we had reached the stage at which the prospects

for achieving some technical improvement looked bright, we explained the situation to the sales division and made sure they understood that our product was now technically superior. The technology and sales divisions then joined forces in carrying out sales activities. The two divisions were able to exchange opinions more openly, and the technical division began to produce a variety of sales aids at the request of the sales division. At the same time, the technical division made the sales division pull up their socks by telling them that they were providing insufficient customer follow-up.

In the first round of sales activities, we found it difficult to get our customers to accept our claims about the technical improvements we had made. They pointed out that we had no results to back up our claims, and our position did not improve. We continued struggling along.

Although top management came down pretty hard on us,

basically they had confidence in me and my staff. This was a great encouragement to us, and at the same time made us feel keenly responsible. We continued to suffer for a while, but at last we found a customer who accepted our explanations, and everybody felt that "this was it." There were some tough conditions attached to this new order, but, with the approval of my bosses, I decided to accept it.

There was an immediate increase in the momentum of our sales activities. The biggest change I noticed was that people who were previously very attached to their own pet technology were now able to take on board customers' opinions with an open mind. By carrying out technical improvements based on our customers' views, we were able to come up with various ideas and achieve the surprising result of reducing the number of faulty parts by 40%.

After the improved equipment was installed, the customer informed us that he was extremely happy to have purchased it. There could have been no better way to encourage our team members, and the number of orders we won rose steadily month by month. As the amount of this kind of work increased, I motivated an experienced engineer by throwing him in at the deep end and letting him take over my role.

If my team members are given opportunities to contact the customer directly, they come to understand their own position well, and, since they can also share in the joy of success with the customer, their work proceeds without my having to say anything.

The competition is fierce and we certainly cannot relax, but we are steadily achieving results and have even received requests for technical collaboration from abroad. I want to make a success of this somehow or other and use it to provide a stimulus to my team members.

As this case study shows, work has various aspects, each requiring a different method of motivation. I want to continue giving each member of my team as many opportunities as possible to contact the world outside the company and have them work at a high level of achievement so they can exercise their full potential as a group.

Case Study 4

A Production Section Manager's Battle Notes

Prologue

The following account concerns a certain production section and is not about the overall management of a company. However, I believe that from the viewpoint of reaching down into people's hearts and bringing out their desire to work, what I have to say applies to any kind of social group.

In January 1965, I was a technical section manager at my company's Kyushu factory and was deeply involved in the construction of a new brine electrolysis plant as part of the development of an 82,000m² green-field site. One day, the production manager called me in and told me I was being transferred.

I was sent off to my new post with the words "It's hard swapping horses in the middle of a race, but I'm afraid you have to go." When I assumed my duties at the Osaka works, the plant manager shocked me when he said that unless the plant was made to pay its way, he couldn't manage it anyhow. And when I called on the production division manager, he flung out that nothing could be done unless sales could be raised.

The section to which I had been transferred was notori-

US$1.00 is approximately equivalent to ¥130 (Dec. 1990)

ous within the company for its uselessness. It produced a high-polymer additive with a monthly turnover of ¥50 million but was running at a loss of ¥5 million per month and also had the company's worst accident record. It had a total of 170 members, nine of whom were technical staff. I was employed for three years in this section, and I put all I had into it and enjoyed the work. By the time I left, I had been able to raise the monthly turnover to ¥100 million, and the section was showing a profit of ¥5 million per month. The section's complement had been reduced to 90. Fortunately, the business climate was improving just at this time during the run-up to the Osaka EXPO and there were manpower shortages, so other sections were able to absorb the personnel made superfluous by our process improvements.

A Production Section Manager's Battle Notes

No Company Goes Bust Because of Shirking Workers

What surprised me most was the workers' apathy in the face of frequent comments about the loss their section was sustaining. While they did not regard themselves as shirking, they thought that nothing could be done about it. They were like beaten dogs whose tails were drooping further and further between their legs. They were putting their energies into union activities as an outlet for their resentment, and this section provided the union with a full-time chief secretary and executive committee members.

In my introductory speech to the section on taking over as manager, I made the following remarks:

"No company has ever gone bankrupt because of its workers shirking. If a company goes bust, it is always because it is badly managed or because its technology is below par. This section has been running in the red for several years, but I do not believe it is because you are slacking. Our competitors are all making a profit, and there is no reason why we cannot do the same. I intend to carry out some drastic improvement, and I would like to have the support of all of you in this. Everyone in this section lacks energy and enthusiasm at the moment, yet everything depends on these factors. Everyone here can work just as hard as those in other sections, and I want to see you all holding your heads high."

During the first two of the three years during which I was in charge of this section, I made the same speech in different words at every morning assembly. As time passed, people stopped looking like whipped curs, and a sparkle gradually came back into their eyes.

The Badger's Coming!

The plant operated on a three-shift system, with the day shift taking over from the night shift at about 7:30 a.m. This was the first time that I had been section manager at a production facility, and I wanted to meet everyone and say hello at least once a day. I also had to learn everybody's names.

I entered the factory gate every morning at 7 a.m. and walked around the plant. Since I had taken over at the beginning of February, it was pitch dark when I left home and a blood-red sun would be burning in the eastern sky as I changed to the Loop Line at Umeda Station. On arriving at the factory, I greeted every individual with a hearty "Good morning. Thank you for your hard work." The startled workers stared after me suspiciously. Their eyes were saying, "What has that new fellow come to do? Has he come to find fault with us?" I even heard some of them whispering, "Watch out! The badger's coming!" I made these tours of the factory every day whatever the weather, even when I had a hangover. After about three months, my "badger" nickname faded away, and more people began to return my greetings. Some of them served me tea, and I even heard that, when I was on a business trip and could not visit the factory, people would ask what had happened to me and wonder whether I was ill.

An unexpected benefit was that my assistant managers came hurrying to the morning meetings, either because they had decided to turn over a new leaf or because they did not want to be outdone by me.

Wringing Out Grumbles

The 170 people in my charge turned up to work each day with long faces, aware of constantly being blamed for losing money for the company. Believing they were bound to have a lot of things to get off their chests, I decided to try listening to their complaints.

There was a system which provided ¥150 per person for after-hours meetings with the workers, and I decided to hold these meetings every week with the day shift. Since we worked a three-shift system, I was able to get around to everybody in three weeks. At the meetings, there were rice crackers and a bowl of noodles and two flasks of grade-two sake per person. I decided to provide any extra sake needed myself. With one of my staff taking minutes, I started off the meetings by describing the present status of our company and section and the progress of the profit improvement plans I had prepared. Then I listened to what everyone had to say. I gave immediate answers whenever possible and initiated action the next day where appropriate. For items requiring discussion, I explained why this was so and postponed them to the following month. This was repeated month after month.

As a result, the number of complaints and expressions of discontent from the workplace gradually decreased. Conversely, the number of constructive opinions expressed increased. Furthermore, the number of accidents gradually declined.

A Central Restroom and Tiled Bathroom

The factory was furnished with restrooms which the workers used for changing their clothes, bathing, and having a smoke. Most of the communal bathtubs installed were old and made of wood. Each of the factory buildings in my section had a small lean-to shed equipped as a restroom. Other sections had a single, large central restroom in their administrative office, but our section still had the old-style facilities —probably because it was failing to make a profit. This led to poor control and inefficient utilization of workers.

I decided to refurbish a nearby empty warehouse and turn it into a central restroom in the name of good labor management and economy. This scheme met with a lot of opposition because it meant that a section operating at a loss was putting forward an investment plan which would increase its financial burden on the company before it had even submitted its plans for making a profit. After taking people's advice, I made the rounds of the personnel, accounting, and sales divisions to prepare the ground, and received permission to start the work. At a cost of ¥5 million, I had a tiled bath installed in the restroom, the first of its kind at the Osaka plant.

The 170 employees in my section were delighted. They probably felt that at last their existence had been recognized, and it appeared that I went up in their esteem.

The next year, when starting on my improvement plans, I had ¥1 million worth of air conditioning put into the restroom, another first at the Osaka works. The first summer after the air conditioning had been installed, the workers from

my section barred entry to people from other sections who
had enviously come to take a look.

40% Investment Efficiency

Since I had contended that my section was losing money because of its inferior technology, I had to provide proof of my
claim. I ordered my nine technical staff members to review
and update the production standards, which had been left
untouched for years, and identify the problem areas in the
existing process. While they were busy with this, I investigated the management situation, main product technology,
and investment status of our competitors over the previous
years.

At the end of the three months, I assembled my nine staff
members together with people from the pure and applied
research divisions, the sales division, and the accounting
division to discuss topics for improvement. As a result, we
started a one-year investigation, with my staff in charge of
performing the necessary experiments. When making my
morning rounds of the factory, I always showed my face in
the laboratory and discussed the progress of the experiments
with each staff member.

Before the year was up, various improvement plans had
been completed. Since the investment was to be in a section
operating at a loss, I decided that we needed a return on investment of 40% rather than the 30% which was usual in the
company. When the amount of investment is reduced in this
way, people come up with ideas to compensate. If an investment return of over 40% was achieved, I used the surplus
to improve the working environment.

As each improvement plan was put into action, the number of workers was cut, our balance of payments improved, and morale rose.

QC Education for Foremen and Team Leaders

I had for some time been convinced that Japan's high educational levels were producing high-quality workers, and I wanted to try giving such people full training in QC and work with them to promote QC on the factory floor.

In 1962, when working in QC section, I was sent to the shop floor from the technical division. My section manager told me to have a go at seeing if the workers could do what I was saying they could. This was my first chance to try effecting workplace improvements together with foremen, team leaders, and workers. We were able to achieve the astonishing result of improving the quality of the final product while saving approximately ¥100 million per year. This gave me tremendous confidence.

Six months later, I was a technical section manager at the Kyushu factory and was planning various operations in connection with the brine electrolysis plant. During this time, I assembled all the factory's foremen and gave them QC education. I had them form study groups in each workplace and made them think about workplace improvement. In the short space of eighteen months, we were able to achieve significant improvements, some of which won company technical awards. The words "QC circle" started to become popular at about this time.

Because of these two experiences, I decided to start QC study groups at the Osaka plant, even with the run-down section of which I was in charge. The first round of seminars was held after work for one hour, with the following curriculum:

A. Awareness of Oneself as Manager
   (During introductory phase, for three months)
   1) Our company and ourselves
   2) The world and ourselves
   3) The history of the dye industry
      (the dye industry in Europe and in Japan)
   4) Ourselves and management
   5) What is unit cost?
   6) Break-even point for profit and loss
B. The Scientific Approach
C. Promoting Our Work
   (During execution phase, for nine months)
   1) Identifying priorities
      (Pareto analysis)
   2) Knowing the status quo
      (graphs, histograms and control charts)
   3) Stratification
   4) Analyzing the status quo
      (cause-and-effect diagrams)
   5) Finding correlations
      (scatter diagrams)

I believed that a grasp of these subjects would be more than adequate to allow improvements to take place. Looking back, I see that the curriculum covered what are now known as the "Seven QC Tools."

It took about a year of one-hour weekly sessions to cover this material. When we reached the QC methods in Part C, I had each class member form a workplace study group to investigate work standards. I then had each person in turn make a verbal report to the others about this process and the results achieved. Although many people disliked talking to a group at first, as time passed they began to speak up on their own initiative.

An informal discussion meeting was held with the plant manager every six months, and I always had the foremen describe the improvement they had achieved at these meetings. Even the plant manager, who used to be scornful of the idea of bringing QC into the workplace and utilizing the knowledge and intelligence of the workers, appeared to become interested in this grass-roots movement.

These group activities, led by foremen and team leaders, made a great contribution to improving our financial position, and our annual profits rose to the ¥100 million level. We also won several company technical awards.

Epilog

My section had continued to operate at a loss for a number of years. Its members were dispirited and the situation was at rock bottom. There was probably no way for it to get any worse. I was able to get all 170 of my section's members to work together with one aim: to tackle the problems and turn the loss into a profit.

When cutting back on the number of workers, I sometimes came into direct conflict with the labor union. Also, as the unit cost fell, the sales division lowered the sales price of the product by an identical amount, and it appeared that our efforts were vanishing into thin air. But the sales volume rose correspondingly, and this in turn decreased the unit cost. In this way, we recovered our profitability.

As I said at the beginning of this report, our monthly turnover doubled and we turned our continual losses into profits. The number of accidents also decreased dramatically. When I left the section, I was overcome by emotion and could not finish my farewell speech. I still have an annual meeting with the foremen and team leaders who helped me during this time, and we have already held more than 20 such gatherings.

Case Study 5

Drawing Out the Wisdom of the Workplace

The case study described here is a report of my experience, as a production-section manager, of a sweeping cost-reduction exercise performed by all my section members on what was our main product model at the time. We started the exercise in April 1985 and achieved our target in September 1986.

The results of our strategy went beyond the attainment of a previously unimaginably high level of cuts in manufacturing costs. Although we achieved a 40% reduction in man-hours (a target on which the company's survival depended), we also created in the process a totally new production system. Everyone concerned played their part to the full and exercised their individuality and cooperative ability in pursuit of our goals. We are now making use of this system and attempting to apply it to other products.

The Latent Power of the Workplace

The first thing I noticed when assigned to the shop floor was the high standard of the workers. The apparent difference between engineers and shop-floor workers had arisen because the workers' experience was not organized systematically and they were only using their skills in a narrow field.

As a result, the workers had a conservative attitude and viewed their individual roles too narrowly.

Because of this workplace ethos, radical improvements planned by engineers often met with only partial success. Here and there, useful ideas for correcting equipment deficiencies went untried because people claimed they were too difficult to implement.

This was the situation when I was given the 40% cost-reduction target mentioned above. To achieve this target, it was imperative to bring out the latent potential of the workers, and some mechanism or other was needed in order to do this.

Setting Up a Mechanism

In setting up the new system, we started by hammering out a clear policy change in which great importance would be given to "group improvement" by QC circles under the slogan "Let's share our skills." To make everyone more aware of problems, we held residential training courses for people from each workplace, taking shop-floor problems as topics of discussion.

We put particular effort into study groups for the next generation of QC circle leaders, describing by means of case studies the value of actual improvements carried out by front-line workers and explaining how problems picked up by such workers can lead to excellent improvements. We also trained people in improvement methods and what to look for by setting practical projects and carrying them out through repeated trial and error. These projects were followed up at regular study meetings with the aim of ensuring that the training produced useful results.

When the people who attended these study meetings had gained some degree of confidence, we announced to all shop-floor employees that everybody would be joining a task team. We then clarified the problems that needed solving, set clear deadlines for their solution, and started group activities.

Task Teams, QC Circles, and the Standing Organization

The group activities were carried out by task teams with three to five members and by team-leader groups formed to open channels of communication among the leaders. Approximately twenty task teams were formed within the production section, and, they proceeded with their activities. The overall organization is a little complicated, but Fig. 2.2 makes it clear. As far as possible, QC circle members from different workplaces facing a particular problem were nominated as task team members.

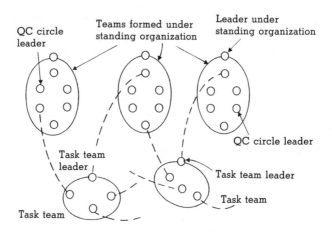

Fig. 2.2 Relation Between Task Teams, Standing Organization and QC Circles

Our objective at the team-leader meetings was to have the team leaders present the results of the analyses performed by their respective teams and their main strategies. In this way, opinions could be exchanged, things could be kept moving in the same general direction, and the areas covered by the various improvement topics could be coordinated. These team-leader meetings were also an arena of competition. By taking technology that had previously been confined to separate individuals or workplaces and making it everyone's common property, cooperation spread rapidly.

To keep more than one iron in the fire, we also decided to continue promoting the existing QC circle activities (which fitted into the standing organization) in conjunction with the new activities. The QC circle activities slackened off for a while because of this, but the new activities gradually began to have a very favorable influence on the topics tackled by the QC circles.

Complete Freedom in Methods

We had all the task teams follow the same method when analyzing the existing situation using IE techniques, and the
same ranking system when working out their priority tasks.
However, they were allowed complete freedom in drawing
up plans for more specific countermeasures, although these
would be modified at the team-leader meetings if they drifted
away from the overall direction in which we were moving.

At first glance, forming task teams like this, apportioning
targets, standards, and deadlines to them, and drawing out
the intelligence of the members by allowing them the freedom to choose their own improvement methods appeared
reckless. However, we decided that it would be possible if
everyone worked together. The outcome was that everyone's
desire to improve the situation increased, study group members held discussions with other groups, and a climate of
friendly competition and opinion exchange emerged. Even
at this stage, the benefits were already becoming apparent.

Analysis of the existing situation showed that most of the
problems to be tackled were in the areas of preparation and
setting-up, and things known as a matter of experience by
the more senior workers were given cast-iron confirmation
by the results of the analysis. This meant that everyone was
able to start on the improvements with confidence in their
analytical results.

When this state of affairs had been achieved, we gradually changed our system of management to one in which we
held regular interim presentation meetings. At these meetings, reports were given, appreciation was shown for people's
efforts, the rewards of achieving good results were shared,

[145]

hints on alternative problem-solving plans were offered, successes were described, and everyone was asked to continue their efforts right up to the final presentation meeting.

The Value of Interim Presentations

While the many interim presentation meetings naturally had the function of controlling the improvement schedule, I noticed that they also facilitated the lateral spread of different kinds of knowledge, made everyone feel the importance of working together toward a common goal, and allowed people to share in and appraise the results obtained.

Something happened at these presentation meetings which surprised everybody. When one leader announced the results of his team's analysis and described the problems and difficulties they were facing, the team leaders from the previous and subsequent processes had everyone's heads nodding in agreement when they in turn pointed out inadequacies in the analytical data and made suggestions for improving it.

Previously, team leaders were thought to be fully occupied just coping with the problems in their own workplaces, but now they had become deeply interested in the processes before and after theirs and even understood them well enough to be able to pick out key improvement points.

When asked how they had come to notice such things, they said that, when setting out to make improvements, they could not possibly ignore the connection between their own process and the previous and subsequent ones. This meant that they had to carefully observe those parts of the previous and subsequent processes which had some bearing on the problems they were facing in their own. After this started happening, the interim presentation meetings became recognized opportunities for helping teams that had become bogged down.

Creating a Partnership System for Cross-Cooperation

Three months after the start of these group activities, a succession of results began to be reported as a result of the groups' efforts. The overall business forecasts improved visibly month by month, and a 33% reduction in man-hours

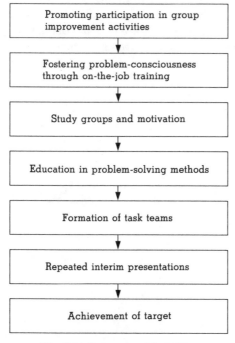

Fig. 2.3 **Sequence of Activities**

(averaged over all processes) was achieved. It took approximately 18 months for the activities to bear fruit from the time when their seeds were first sown. Fig. 2.3 shows the various stages in this process.

To make these group activities applicable to other products, we are now reviewing them and starting to run them as part of the standing organization. Things have been arranged to foster close cooperation among people from different areas and enable people to experience a wide range of work. The task team setup is also being used as a temporary organization for new models.

Everybody is helping to create an effective partnership system that makes full use of everyone's human qualities and is based on respect for different ideas. Using this system, we are continuing to tackle various problems.

Case Study 6

Making Use of Teamwork

Introduction

The equipment used in a steelworks can be divided into three main groups; iron-making equipment, steel-making equipment and rolling equipment. Because of this, the technology employed has also been split up for convenience into three classes; iron-making technology, steel-making technology, and rolling technology. Competition is apt to take precedence over cooperation among the different technical areas, conflict of opinion often arises, and mutual understanding does not always prevail.

This was the situation when I was working at the Hirohata Steelworks of Nippon Steel Corporation and Professor K visited us to advise on quality control. Just at that time, we had a quality problem concerning surface defects on steel plate.

Surface Defects on Steel Plate

Fig. 2.4 shows the plate production process. Molten iron from the blast furnace is converted to steel in the converter, and the molten steel is then formed into slabs by ingot making or continuous casting. The slab is then rolled to form steel

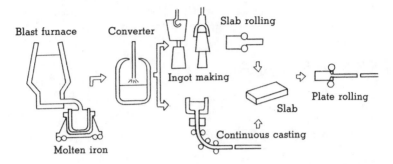

Fig. 2.4 Process Diagram for Production of Steel Plate

plate. The iron-making division is responsible for the process up until the formation of the molten iron; the steel-making division for the intermediate stage up to the formation of the ingots or the completion of continuous casting; and the rolling division for the subsequent slabbing and rolling processes.

In the steel-making process, technical priority is given to controlling the composition of the steel; but in the rolling process, greatest importance is placed on the quality of the material and the shape of the product. This meant that the problem of surface defects on the product tended to fall in a technical blind spot, since it straddled both divisions. Instead of mounting a serious investigation of the causes, we were prone to avoiding the problem by treating the symptoms, i.e., by repairing the defects. It was therefore taken for granted that surface defects had to be removed, and this process for slab and plate was included in the production process as a matter of course.

The rolling division classified the different types of surface defects by appearance (i.e., by shape) rather than by cause. Priority was given to developing efficient slab repair

[150]

methods, and surface defects were treated as chronic and unavoidable.

Measures for Reducing Slab Defects

Even when the surface of a slab was removed, traces of the defects would sometimes remain on the final product (i.e., the plate), necessitating a further repair operation. Gradually, attention began to be focused on the following two problems arising from this:

1) Poor external appearance of the product.
2) Increased costs arising from the repair work, which had to be carried out off-line.

A campaign was started with the aim of halving the repair work. Since 50% of the surface defects to steel plates resulted from slab surface defects, we had to start by reducing these slab defects.

From their appearance, defects could be classified into two main types: cracking, in which cracks appeared on the surface, and scabbing, in which parts of the surface peeled off after the plate had been rolled. Particular attention was focused on these.

Groups were immediately formed to devise ways of reducing the plate and slab defects, and the reasons for the occurrence of the slab defects were investigated and analyzed based on existing observations, technology, and countermeasures. As a result, problems such as the following were uncovered:

1) Although the root causes of slab defects and the factors promoting them were diverse and complexly interrelated, previous investigations had concentrated on isolated, individual countermeasures.

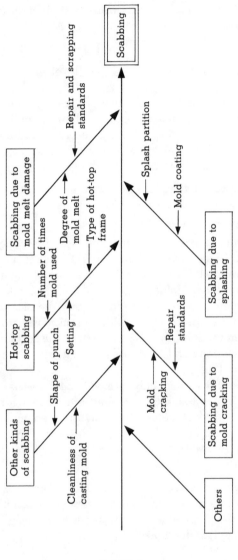

Fig. 2.5 Cause-and-Effect Diagram for Scabbing

2) Although the degree of care and attention to detail exercised while working greatly affected the nature and frequency of occurrence of the defects, it was difficult to identify the quality of work in one's own process.
3) The positioning of quality among the workplace control items was unclear.

To solve these problems, it was necessary to discover an effective combination of measures to halve the defects over the whole process from steel-making to slab finishing. Fig. 2.5 is a cause-and-effect diagram for scabbing as one example of a slab defect.

Our staff group then drew up a program of experiments using standard procedures; four shop tests were performed, and the relative contribution of each factor to the defects was measured.

Establishing a Quality Control System

Since we now had a rough idea of the cause-and-effect relationship behind the defects, we had to improve our performance by making use of the findings in our actual work while investigating the problem in further detail. This required organized activities throughout the long process from steel-making to slab finishing, so we started by preparing a detailed QC process chart.

There was already an active program of autonomous control activities of workers at the Hirohata Works, and a system enabling the workers to achieve clearly set targets through their own efforts had been cultivated for some time. As pointed out by Professor K, any measures taken to reduce defects would depend largely on the skills of the shop-floor workers. As much responsibility as possible was therefore

[153]

Mold Maintenance Checksheet

									Stamp				Section manager	Foreman	Group leader
													Quality assurance inspector	Mold setter	

Check items	Mold no.	Number of times used	Condition of internal faces of mold					Checked by	Time	Ingot no. 1	2	3	4	5	6	7	8	9	10	11
Month day shift																				
			Long side	East		Name Ope-rator	During setting													
				West		"	After setting													
			Short side	South		"	Before setting													
				North		"	"													
							"				Centering Dis-placement Clearance	Centering Dis-placement Clearance	Centering Dis-placement Clearance	Centering Dis-placement Clearance	Centering Dis-placement Clearance	Centering Dis-placement Clearance	Centering Dis-placement Clearance	Centering Dis-placement Clearance	Centering Dis-placement Clearance	Centering Dis-placement Clearance
											Effective/ Ineffective	Effective/ Ineffective	Effective/ Ineffective	Effective/ Ineffective	Effective/ Ineffective	Effective/ Ineffective	Effective/ Ineffective	Effective/ Ineffective	Effective/ Ineffective	Effective/ Ineffective
7										Pass/ fail	Pass/ fail	Pass/ fail	Pass/ fail	Pass/ fail	Pass/ fail	Pass/ fail	Pass/ fail	Pass/ fail	Pass/ fail	Pass/ fail

Control test no. — Steel grade — Charge number — Cart no. — Type of mold — Group no. — Coating type

Fig. 2.6 Checksheet

[154]

given to the people actually doing the work, and a control system directly linked to the workplace was established. The key points of this system were as follows:

1) The control system was built around the foremen in each workplace.
2) Surface defects were classified into sixteen different types according to the causes.
3) The results produced by each process were reliably identified.
4) Improvement was accelerated by increasing the speed with which the quality of the product was followed up.

We also introduced the following documentation to support the system:

1) Ingot-Making Quality Assurance Checksheets (See Fig. 2.6)
2) Quality Follow-Up Cards (See Fig. 2.7)
3) Control charts

The aims of the Ingot-Making Quality Assurance Checksheets were as follows:

1) To clarify the quality assurance check items in each process.
2) To enable the workers themselves to check the results of their work.
3) To nominate the person responsible for quality assurance for each job.
4) To double-check the results of the previous process.

The Quality Follow-Up Cards communicated information about quality abnormalities between the steel-making plant and the rolling mill. They were used for checking the results of the work, performing investigations for workplace quality improvement experiments, making requests to deal with

Part 2: MOTIVATION IN INDUSTRY

Quality Follow-Up Card $(\frac{1}{2}$ Ingot-making $-$ Slabbing   No. [   ]

Subject								Originators		
								Work-place	Com-pleted by	Group leader
Date of issue	Day		Month		Year		Shift Group			
			Mold	Mold sand	After pouring					
					Top pouring	Bottom pouring				

	Results of operation	Temporary countermeasure

Investigation and corrective actions	Year Month Day Shift Group	Workplace	Completed by	Group leader

(Top surface)   (Bottom surface)

T   B   T   B

Hot scarfing (Y/N)
H Finishing temperature
Furnace retention time

Notes								

Checked by originators	Completed by	Group leader	Foreman	Supervisor	

Fig. 2.7   Quality Follow-up Card

Making Use of Teamwork

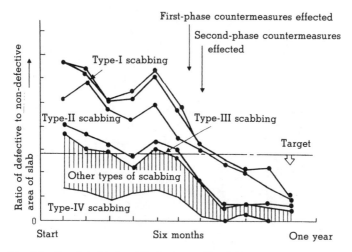

Fig. 2.8 Trend in Ratio of Defective to Non-Defective Area of Slab

work outside the technical standards, etc. The main features of the cards were as follows:

1) Direct communication between workplaces.
2) Feedback always provided to the originator.

As a result of these measures, we obtained the unexpectedly good results shown in Fig. 2.8 and were able to attain our targets in about a year.

Summary

In the countermeasures described here, priority was given to inculcating the idea that the workers themselves should improve their processes based on rapid feedback of product

[157]

quality information from the subsequent processes. This mechanism made it possible to take rapid action to eliminate the root causes if the problem of surface defects reappeared, and we were therefore able to obtain the anticipated results.

A particularly noteworthy point was that quality problems straddling different divisions and plants, which had previously tended to fall in a blind spot, were gradually resolved. This was a result of the natural improvement in teamwork between divisions and plants and the clarification of the responsibility of each workplace produced by adopting a control system directly linked to the workplace.

The know-how thus accumulated gradually evolved into the technology required for producing defect-free slabs and helped to lay the foundations for the combined steel-making and rolling system presently being introduced.

Case Study 7

Starting Up QC Circles

Introduction

From 1954 to 1962, I was engaged in creating a quality control system for a certain large factory. In those days, people were not attracted by the mention of QC like they are today. Top management showed no interest, saying, "That's what we've been doing all along, isn't it?", while labor unions simply opposed it without even trying to find out what it was.

When I moved to my company's technical division in 1954, I was told to create a system of work standards. I could not object to this, since I had previously taken some basic quality control courses, starting with a three-day course held at the Osaka Chamber of Commerce and Industry the day after a big typhoon struck in 1950. I spent my company's money and made people envious of me because of this rare opportunity to escape from my normal place of work.

To carry out QC, which at that time was menaced by enemies on all sides, one's first duty was to make top management see why work standards were necessary. I was very concerned, because I knew I had to create a system of standards that would be accepted by those above me as well as by those below me. I thought up the following rationale:

"Work standardization lets engineers hand over workplace

control to the workers, allowing engineers to concentrate on developing and improving technology. This enables us to build a system with which we can beat our competitors in the future."

I avoided the term "QC," using the word "standardization" instead. I remember the journal of the Japanese Standards Association at that time was called "JIS." Over the next eight years, we created a factory-wide organization more complex even than the labor union in the name of "standardization" and used this to institute a system for preparing and executing a variety of standards and regulations including production standards (technical standards), work standards, specifications, standard test methods, design standards, and preventive maintenance regulations.

Next, when we began standardizing man-hours and started to get into the area of industrial engineering, I was told to get out onto the shop-floor. This was how I took my leave of my eight years' work on standardization, etc.

Try It and See!

In the summer of 1962, I returned to the factory floor. After so many years of wearing a suit and tie, I breathed a sigh of relief. When I went to meet my new section manager, he said, "You say that workers can manage their own workplace through standardization. Try it and see if they really can." He thought that the workplace could only be managed by technical specialists. After all, that was how he himself had worked his way up to his present position.

Trying Out My Ideas on QC

My section manager was not ill-disposed. He simply thought that ordinary workers were incapable of managing themselves and that that was what he and the other engineers were there for. To surprise him, I had to choose an improvement topic which would give striking results.

(1) Choosing a topic

Where engineers are concerned, raising the yield of a process is the best kind of improvement. I therefore prepared a Pareto diagram using the following formula:

(maximum theoretical yield − average actual yield) × production volume × unit cost

After examining the Pareto diagram prepared for the fifty different types of dye intermediates which my section was in charge of producing, and taking into account the relative difficulty of effecting improvements, I selected the second intermediate product in the process as the target of our improvement drive.

[161]

(2) Every worker has his own private work standards

The next thing was to find out all about the workplace, so I toured the shop floor every day talking to the workers. Mainly, I asked them what they paid most attention to while they were working, and I discovered that everyone had his or her own private work standards, which differed from the official company standards. I decided to find out whose work had the best effect on the yield. To do this, I prepared graphs of the yield stratified according to worker, shift, and process. Of course, the result was not absolutely clear-cut, but the yield appeared to be best when a certain Mr. O was in charge of a specific job in a particular process.

What was more surprising was that, after I had started making my rounds of the workplace, the yield slowly but surely began to improve by itself.

(3) Preparing work standards together

Two months had passed since I had started this job. I now knew that each employee had his or her own individual work standards.

I began to think that, rather than imposing the company standards, I would try getting everyone to cooperate in preparing standards which all would obey. I believed that everyone would be bound to follow standards which they themselves had set.

I prepared a questionnaire and had everyone fill in the following items in the order in which the work was performed:

* Working conditions observed
* Span of control
* Things to which most attention is paid
* Work which one has to be extra careful about (with reasons)
* Things which one must not do (with reasons)

* Points to note when handing over to the next process
* Points to note when handing over to the next shift

This survey was completed over a period of two weeks.

I also assembled the workers after work and used graphs and control charts of the yield to explain that, if the process variation could be reduced, the average yield would be bound to rise. I kept on repeating this until everyone was convinced. As everyone began to review their work and think about what they were doing, the yield again rose by itself.

Two weeks later, when everyone had handed in their forms, I received a pleasant surprise. Without discussing their intentions with anyone, the workers had filled in on their forms their own private work standards.

I prepared a chart showing everyone's work standards and held meetings with each shift. Everyone was surprised at the discrepancies among their personal work standards. I told them that I thought the reason for the variation in yield probably lay in the differences in the standards, and everyone readily agreed.

I then showed them the graphs stratified by worker, shift, and process which I had prepared earlier, and we discussed what should be done. There were about five people on each shift. I patiently guided the discussion in the direction of Mr. O's work procedures. There was no need to rush things, since the yield was increasing by itself anyway. The meetings were held at a relaxed pace for one hour every other day after work, extending over a month. Since we were not allowed to drink at the meetings, tea and cookies were provided. Thankfully, nobody objected and everybody seemed happy to take part.

Work standards had to be sanctioned by the production section manager. I obtained his consent to the work standards we had prepared together and posted them in the workplace.

I also put up graphs of the yield. The yield rose and settled at a high point on the control chart, and the variation of course decreased.

As the yield rose, product quality improved, which in turn improved the yield and quality of the intermediate produced in the next process. The production section manager was delighted. A further benefit was that dyes made from the intermediate produced in the next process became deeper and more brilliant in hue.

The extra profit generated by the improvement in this intermediate amounted to around ¥100 million per year. I was satisfied that this was the "workplace QC" I had been dreaming of.

The Production Section Manager Is Suitably Impressed

While all this was going on, my section manager had been viewing our activities with suspicion. He thought that raising yields was by its very nature the job of engineers, and not something that workers could do. That was precisely why engineers were engineers and workers were workers.

It was not as if I was doing some amazing experiment as he thought. I simply walked around the shop floor about twice a day, occasionally drew up some graphs, and sometimes got the workers together for lively discussions. Even so, the yield rose month by month. In addition, the yield and quality of the intermediate produced in the next process improved and the dyes in which this intermediate was used increased in brilliance and depth. The section manager was extremely impressed. I told him that these were the benefits of stan-

---

US$1.00 is approximately equivalent to ¥130. (Dec. 1990)

dardization, and that from now on it was up to the engineers. I asked him to carry out lots of experiments.

This production section manager was a fighter who, while I had been working in the technical division drawing up standards, had been battling to completely eliminate moisture from the raw materials that his section used. He became a believer in the kind of standardization which I was aiming at, and, even after I left, he followed my methods and continued steadily raising the yields of the products his section was producing.

The Division Manager Fails to Understand

By raising the yields and quality of our intermediates and dyes, we had increased our annual profits by approximately ¥100 million and were therefore justified in claiming a major technical achievement. I approached my division manager, believing that we should apply for a technical award in the company.

He knew what I was going to say before I had even opened my mouth. Haughtily, he said, "It's a good result. But what on earth have my managers been playing at up till now? This is exactly what we should have been doing all along. It certainly can't be called technology. If I put this up at the awards conference, I'll be laughed out of court."

His words showed that he did not understand the value of control. He was also a sad case of a manager who did not know how to use praise in motivating people. I talked to my section manager, and the two of us showed our appreciation to the foreman and workers who had cooperated in this project.

Reforming the Production Standards

Based on the work standards which the workers had prepared together, I reformed the technical production standards. In the space provided for the authors' names, I listed all the names of the fifteen or so workers who had helped in preparing the standards. This was the least I could do to show how I felt, and it was also a way of venting my defiance toward the production division manager.

Conclusion

Although this happened in the days before QC circles existed, we cannot deny that it was a QC circle type of activity. It was a group activity in which workers were organized to create standards. The story shows that group activities always need a good leader, and this is true whether one is running a country, a company, or a small workplace like the one described here.

I worked in this section for half a year. At the end, the workers with whom I had spent these six months organized a dinner party for me and gave me a heartfelt send-off. The foreman at that time continued to make a succession of improvements to the workplace and became known as "Mr. Circle." He still sends me a New Year card every year even though he has retired, and this year's card announced that he was practicing QC in his senior citizens' club!

APPENDIX

Human Motivation Study Course

Our Changing Times

As we enter the 1990s, the times are changing and new trends are emerging.

The Motivation Research Group was inaugurated in February 1974—directly after the first energy crisis—under the leadership of Professor Yoshio Kondo at the instigation of Dr. Eizaburo Nishibori.

The 1980s were a time of bewildering change as the era of high economic growth drew to a close and the low-growth era began. Industry restructured, shifting its emphasis from heavy engineering to smaller and lighter products. The proportion of middle-aged and older people in the population increased, and Japan became more internationally aware with the yen's surge in value. Public corporations came to a dead-end and were privatized, stockpiled goods increased, and production and distribution were improved. The Japanese economy began to change direction from being export-oriented to being more concerned with domestic demand, and business conditions improved as domestic demand expanded.

Important Topics in Motivation

These changes also produced large changes in the areas of greatest concern to motivation. In the high-growth era, motivation was generally considered to be a blue-collar problem or a problem of youth. After the first energy crisis and the subsequent changes in the structure of manufacturing industry, the problem started to become one of white-collar workers and people of middle and older age. Managers and staff who had previously talked about motivation as a problem concerning others, not themselves, now found it was their own problem.

As we enter the 1990s, business is becoming more international. Job reforms and structural changes are proceeding apace, the population's age distribution continues to shift to the higher end of the scale, and a fresh crop of motivation problems is beginning to surface. Autonomy and independence are now demanded of the people who have until now been discussing the problems of motivation from within the sheltering arms of their corporations. They are now required to take full responsibility for themselves. Whether they remain within their established organizations and take charge of new business projects or leave their companies to undertake new experiences, they are still required to be self-reliant.

Response to Change

In the midst of the structural changes which industry is undergoing, industrial corporations are also changing in the search for ways to prolong their existence. During this process, they require that their employees be able to respond to change as well.

According to Dr. S. Sanuki, a specialist in aeronautical engineering and former professor at the University of Tokyo, mankind was able to take to the sky not by demanding stability in the air but rather by sacrificing stability for maneuverability. Stability and maneuverability are mutually contradictory, and instability in itself leads to maneuverability; the more maneuverable airplanes were made, the safer they became.

Before the advent of the Wright brothers, aircraft designers gave top priority to stability in their designs. This was acceptable when there were only small movements in the air currents, but such designs failed when violent changes occurred because they were unable to respond. The Wright brothers stopped searching for stability and pursued a design which, though unstable, gave sufficient maneuverability to overcome this disadvantage. This was the secret of their success.

In times of great change, the people who matter will not be those who search for stability, but those who can accept instability and are flexible enough to find their own balance.

New Needs

Corporations undertake the following actions:

(1) They promote internationalization.
(2) They develop new areas of business.
(3) They put resources into research and development.
(4) They place importance on marketing and sales activities.

Because of this, they also do the following:

(5) They require their employees to be able to respond to change.

In future, the problem of motivation will be how to respond to these corporate needs and at the same time satisfy individual needs.

Professor Kondo makes the following claim:

APPENDIX

"The basis for motivation is recognizing and exercising the human factors in work, particularly creativity and sociality. This will probably remain unchanged as long as mankind exists on the earth, irrespective of race or locality. However, the priorities at which motivation is directed will change along with today's rapidly-changing world conditions."

How should we promote the kind of motivation which will answer these demands in the future? The Human Motivation Study Course described below is aimed at meeting these demands in full.

Human Motivation Study Course

The motivation study course presented here was researched and developed over a period of more than three years by the Japanese Standards Association's Motivation Research Group. It is a unique program founded on the pioneering spirit of Dr. Nishibori, the logical approach of Professor Kondo, and the practical experiences of the Motivation Research Group's members in their companies (see Fig. 1). The inspiration behind the course is the pioneering spirit of Dr. Nishibori, and it incorporates the theory and practice of disciplines such as psychology, behavioral science, management science, and QC.

In his career as an engineer, Dr. Nishibori helped to promote technical development and to pioneer QC in Japan. He has also contributed to the development of atomic energy utilization as Executive Director of the Japan Atomic Energy Research Institute. Through the Japanese Standards Association, he has also worked on new-product development and creativity development.

As a senior member of the Academic Alpine Club of Kyoto University and President of the Japanese Alpine Club, Dr.

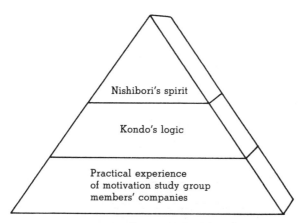

Fig. 1 Components of Human Motivation Training

Nishibori has succeeded in conquering several previously untrodden peaks. He also solved many new and unfamiliar problems in leading The Japanese Antarctic Research Expedition (JARE) to success.

Through experiences such as these, Dr. Nishibori has developed great determination and strength of character. Furthermore, he has built himself a career not as an academician or scientist but as an engineer. The rational approach has enabled him to give us invaluable teachings which appeal to more than the emotions alone.

Based as it is on these achievements, Dr. Nishibori's philosophy is an invaluable guide for businessmen and engineers in the future.

Motivation Systems

Stimulating people's desire to act, i.e., motivating them, is

APPENDIX

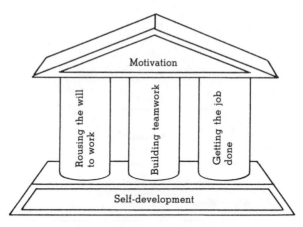

Fig. 2 Structure of Human Motivation Training

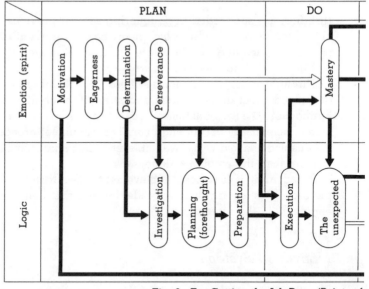

Fig. 3 For Getting the Job Done (Points of

[174]

something managers and supervisors should do through on-the-job training as a matter of daily routine. But, while motivating people is extremely important, it is by no means easy.

The Motivation Research Group's Human Motivation Study Course aims to help people study motivation through on-the-job training and find out what they must do in order to practice it more effectively.

The course presents the structure of motivation as a large roof resting on three pillars mounted on a solid base (see Fig. 2). The base represents self-development. If we are to motivate our subordinates and team members and occasionally our superiors or senior colleagues, we must first motivate ourselves.

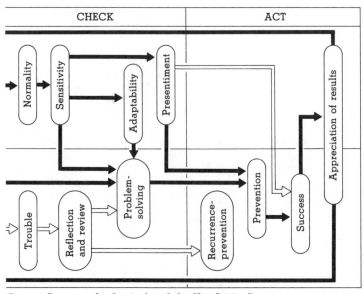

Contact Between the Logical and the Non-Logical)

APPENDIX

Three large pillars stand on this firm base. The first pillar is "getting the job done" (see Fig. 3). This means working out how to proceed in order to complete a large or difficult task. The second pillar is "building teamwork." We do not usually slave away in isolation, but work together with others with the aim of achieving a common purpose. Teamwork is vital. The third pillar is "rousing the will to work." This means giving people the desire to do something, and it applies to oneself as well as to one's subordinates and team members. These three pillars support the roof representing motivation, and this is the structure of our motivation study course.

Table 1. A Methodology of Motivation

	The 3 Pillars	The 7 Tools (Key Steps)
Reform Oneself (Self-Motivation)	Getting the Job Done Achieving Targets	(1) Decide to do the project. (2) Create a sense of urgency—the project *must* be accomplished. (3) Think positively—be convinced of success. (4) Investigate and prepare thoroughly. (5) Draw on people's inner resources and give freedom in methods. (6) Be prepared for the unexpected to happen. (7) Reflect on progress and turn disasters into successes.
	Building Teamwork Participation and Cooperation	(1) Give everyone a common purpose. (2) Allocate roles and impart a sense of mission. (3) Work together with respect for each other's differences. (4) Be aware that no one is perfect. (5) Act with love. (6) "Reach out." (7) Compete fairly without quarreling.
Self-Development	Rousing the Will to Work Raising Morale	(1) Treat team members' individuality as their strength. (2) Listen to what everyone has to say. (3) Clarify your goals. (4) Give your team members opportunities to prove themselves. (5) Encourage your team members. (6) Treat everyone fairly. (7) Take responsibility in advance.

Motivation is affected by a multiplicity of different factors and requires various responses depending on person, time, and place. However, these factors include some basic, universal ones, and the structure described above was derived from analysis and discussion of these.

Motivation Methods

In this study course, each of the three pillars of motivation has been broken down into seven key points to provide a methodology. We call these key points the "seven tools" (see Table 1).

The seven tools or key steps for the first pillar ("getting the job done") are as follows:

(1) Decide to do the project.
(2) Create a sense of urgency—the project must be accomplished.
(3) Think positively—be convinced of success.
(4) Investigate and prepare thoroughly.
(5) Draw on people's inner resources and give freedom in methods.
(6) Be prepared for the unexpected to happen.
(7) Reflect on progress and turn disasters into successes.

The seven tools or key steps in the second pillar, "building teamwork" (i.e., participation and cooperation) are as follows:

(1) Give everyone a common purpose.
(2) Allocate roles and impart a sense of mission.
(3) Work together with respect for each other's differences.
(4) Be aware that no one is perfect.

(5) Act with love.

(6) Reach out.

(7) Compete fairly without quarreling.

The seven tools or key steps which make up the third pillar are as follows:

(1) Treat team members' individuality as their strength.

(2) Listen to what everyone has to say.

(3) Clarify the goals.

(4) Give the team members opportunities to prove themselves.

(5) Encourage the team members.

(6) Treat everyone fairly.

(7) Take responsibility in advance.

Each of the seven tools or key steps which make up the three pillars has its own significance. They are scrutinized and discussed carefully during the training so as to deepen students' understanding and acceptance of them.

Practicing these key points will enable us to master the secrets of the top motivators.

Carrying Out the Training

The danger with motivation training is that, if done clumsily, the very things which should foster a positive, active attitude do exactly the opposite and create a negative, passive outlook. When people hear inspiring words from an authority figure such as a manager, a religious leader or a sports coach, the more they nod their heads obediently, the stronger becomes the superior-subordinate relationship between speaker and listeners. Before they realize it, the listeners have lost their autonomy and freedom of action.

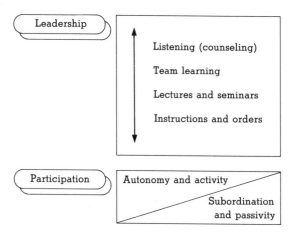

Fig. 4 Leadership and Membership

In company management, the most direct method is simply to issue orders and instructions, creating a relationship of complete dominance and submission between those in positions of authority and their subordinates. At the opposite extreme lies "listening" (or "counseling"), the least direct method. In this method, managers listen carefully to their subordinates and a relationship of independence and freedom grows up between them. This is an effective way of bringing out people's positivity and initiative.

Training can be performed in various styles. In our Human Motivation Study Course, we avoid lectures and instruction as far as possible, concentrating on discussions among the participants. The training is carried out in groups from start to finish (see Fig. 4).

Although the training takes place mainly through group discussion, allowing the discussion to flow freely with nothing concrete to hold onto sometimes becomes pure laissez-faire; people simply talk about what they like, and no good results are obtained. Materials are therefore prepared in order to give some direction to the discussion.

Training by the group discussion method using such materials is known as Instrumented Team Learning (ITL) (see Table 2). The kinds of materials used in our course are as follows:

Topic:
Provides participants with an indication of what to discuss.

Text:
Read aloud by students; gives direction to group discussions and suggests topics to talk about.

Worksheets:
Gets students working (writing, drawing, calculating, etc.) along the lines suggested by the topic.

Study Materials:
Not used during training periods but handed out for students to take away and study in order to deepen their understanding. These materials are not given out in the form of complete textbooks but are distributed in sequence as small leaflets or loose sheets. The object of this is to increase the participants' degree of concentration on the training.

There are various methods of holding group discussions, but ours has certain special features. In the Human Motivation Study Course, we aim at achieving the following kinds of mutual development benefits through group discussion:

(1) Deeper understanding of the learning materials.
(2) Exchange of opinion.
(3) Sharing of experience.

Table 2 Human Motivation Training by Instrumented Team Learning

Instrumented (based on learning materials)	Dr. Nishibori's pioneering spirit Professor Kondo's theoretical research Practical Activities at Motivation Research Group Members' Companies
Team (mutual development: team learning) Learning	Participants: Understanding of learning materials Opinion exchange Experience sharing

Our aim is definitely not to try to reach any hard-and-fast conclusions.

As mentioned earlier, motivation is composed of a variety of different elements and is a profound subject when treated in depth. It is not simply a matter of finding a single best solution. It is important not to search impatiently for conclusions but to deepen one's thinking through repeated rumination.

Participants therefore discuss the elements of motivation, but they do not produce any conclusions as a group. Their motivation skills are increased by bearing in mind what they have talked about, recalling it when actually practicing motivation, and taking their thinking even deeper.

In this course, the lecturers do not say to the students, "This is how you should motivate." The course has been devised with the aim of allowing them, through their training, to master this by themselves.

Sekishu Katagiri, founder of the Sekishu tea ceremony school and builder of the Zen temple Jiko-In in Nara, said, "The tea ceremony cannot be transmitted directly from master to students. It must be learned through observation of its methods and discussion of its principles by the students themselves. It cannot be taught by writing books."

[181]

APPENDIX

Our Human Motivation Study Course has much in common with the Sekishu method. The participants are made to think, state their opinions, and hold group discussions in order to learn for themselves. Sekishu taught using the catechetical method between master and students, but in the Human Motivation Study Course, the students talk among themselves. Learning what motivation is all about is not easy. It should be acquired by the learners themselves, not by relying on a teacher but by standing on their own feet.

We never forget the things we ourselves have worked hard to master, but we soon forget the things others have taught us.

Based on this philosophy, we supplement the group discussions in the course by training in self-control techniques such as tension and relaxation exercises, abdominal breathing, learning to feel warmth and massiveness, and Chevreal's pendulum. Mastering these techniques enables a person to relax or concentrate at will. Various exercises on topics such as mastering the arts of listening and communicating and linking this to improvement effort are also built into the curriculum.

We have no hesitation in recommending this course, the curriculum for which is shown in Table 3. Those interested may obtain further details from the seminars section at the Kansai Branch of the Japanese Standards Association.

Table 3 The Human Motivation Study Course

	Day 1	Day 2	Day 3
9:30	Orientation		Explanation
	1. Self-development Self-introductions Preliminary survey Reading aloud Communicating and listening	(GD) Reflection and revision (GD) Seven Tools for Getting the Work Done	4. Raising Morale (Rousing the Will to Work) (GD) Respect for Individuality
	(GD) Stress and Relaxation (GD) TQC for Management	3. Participation and Cooperation (GD) The Purpose and Role of Cooperation (1) (GD) The Purpose and Role of Cooperation (2) (GD) Why Do We Work? Information transmis- sion game (1) (GD) Review of infor- mation transmission game (1)	(GD) Targets Should be Set by Those Respon- sible for Achieving Them (GD) Free Choice in Methods (GD) Give People Opportunities and Get Them Going
12:30		Explanation	
13:30	2. Achieving Targets (GD) Nothing Ventured, Nothing Gained (GD) Impart a sense of urgency (GD) Draw on Every- one's Expertise (GD) Believe in Success (GD) Decide to Start, Then Investigate (GD) Prepare Thoroughly (GD) Be Prepared for the Unexpected (GD) Act According to Circumstances	Information transmission game (2) (GD) Review of infor- mation transmission game (2) (GD) Communication (GD) Cooperation (GD) Act with Love (GD) Reach Out (GD) Fair Competition, not Quarreling (GD) The 7 Tools for Teamwork	(GD) Encouragement (GD) The Spirit of Fair Play Tension and Relaxa- tion–Chevreal's Pendulum (GD) Taking Responsi- bility (GD) The 7 Tools for Rousing the Will to Work Final Survey Course Impressions Questionnaires
17:30	(GD) Be Resolved		End

* (GD = Group Discussion)

[183]

Bibliography

Deming W.E. (1980), "Some Obstacles to Improvement in Quality and Efficiency," Erfaringer fra Kvalitatsstyring I Japan, p. 87.

Herzberg, F. (1969), "The Motivation to Work," John Wiley and Sons, New York.

Juran, J.M. (1973), "The Taylor System and Quality Control," Quality Progress, vol. 6, May, p. 42.

Kondo, Y. (1975), "Work, Sports, QC Circle," FQC, No. 141, p. 33 (Japanese).

———. (1977), "Creativity in Daily Work," 1977 ASQC Technical Conference Transactions—Philadelphia, p. 430.

———. (1981), "Participation and Leadership," 1981-ASQC Quality Congress Transactions—San Francisco, p. 110.

———. (1986), "Human Motivation and Achievement of Work—A Report of Motivation Study Group, JSA—," Transactions of 30th EOQC Conference, Stockholm 1986, p. 409.

———. (1989), "Improvement of Productivity Versus Humanity," Human Systems Management, vol. 8, p. 23.

Maslow, A.H. (1953), "A Theory of Human Motivation," Psychological Review, vol. 50, p. 370.

McGregor, D. (1960), "The Human Side of Enterprise," McGraw-Hill, New York.

Nishibori, E.E. (1971), "Humanity and Development of Creativity," Japan Productivity Center, Tokyo (Japanese).

Okusa, F. (1985), "TQC—For What Purpose?," Hinshitsu Kanri (Total Quality Control), vol. 36, p. 88 (Japanese).

BIBLIOGRAPHY

O'Toole, J. et al. (1973), "Work in America," MIT Press, Cambridge, MA, p. 3.

Tokizane T. (1970), "Ningen de Aru Koto" ("Being Human"), Iwanami Publishing Co., Tokyo.